PRO CHRISTO ET ECCLESIA

Ex Libris

BRYAN F. SPINNEY

CONTEMPORARY PARISH PRAYERS

CONTEMPORARY PARISH PRAYERS

Compiled and edited
by
FRANK COLQUHOUN

With a Foreword by
THE ARCHBISHOP OF CANTERBURY

HODDER AND STOUGHTON
LONDON SYDNEY AUCKLAND TORONTO

In grateful memory of
my Mother
VIOLET MILBOROUGH COLQUHOUN
(1878–1970)
who first taught me to pray

CONTENTS

CONTENTS

III PRAYERS FOR PARISH OCCASIONS

FOREWORD
BY THE ARCHBISHOP OF CANTERBURY

THE composition of prayers in the modern idiom is no easy task. To avoid the chatty and the cheap, to write with dignity and a sense of awe, this is an ideal difficult of achievement. Many have recently attempted to do this—and failed.

Canon Colquhoun, whose former book of *Parish Prayers* has been widely appreciated, has here provided a book which goes a long way to meet the needs of those who want to pray in twentieth-century language. We may regard it as a step forward along a difficult path, and an aid to those who, using modern liturgies, wish to match them with prayers written in a similar idiom.

It was my privilege to write a Foreword to *Parish Prayers*, and I am glad to do so for this new book. I wish it well in the service and worship of the Lord of the Church.

DONALD CANTUAR:

January 1975

AUTHOR'S PREFACE

THIS collection of prayers is intended to serve as a companion to my *Parish Prayers*, published in 1967. Though not designed on so extensive a scale as its predecessor it covers much the same ground and has a similar purpose in view: to provide a comprehensive manual of prayers for use at parish level.

Dr. Donald Coggan has once again done me the honour of contributing the foreword, this time in his capacity as Archbishop of Canterbury. In expressing my sincere thanks to him I wish to say how greatly I value not only the generous words he has written but also the interest he has shown in this new undertaking.

In the short interval that has elapsed since *Parish Prayers* was issued there has been an increasing demand for prayers in "modern" rather than traditional idiom, avoiding the archaic and sometimes artificial phraseology of the past and employing a simpler and more natural form of speech. This, I am sure, is good. At the same time I am convinced that prayers intended for use in public worship must possess a certain beauty and dignity, a sense of reverence and wonder in the presence of God the all-holy. The Series 3 forms of service in our own Church are seeking to establish a standard in this direction. The prayers in this book follow much the same pattern, though some of them go a step further in the direction of modern language and are more akin to our normal everyday speech.

On the whole subject of contemporary prayer little more need be said here; yet it is strange that many good church people still resist any change in the language of Christian devotion and appear to think that there is something disrespectful in addressing God as *you* instead of in terms of *thee* and *thou*. They argue that we should not speak to the Almighty in the same way that we talk to our fellow men. But clearly such an argument will not bear serious examination. It overlooks the fact that 300 or 400 years ago *thee* and *thou* was the customary form of address to man as well as to God. The evidence of the Book of Common Prayer and the Authorized Version of the Bible makes this plain. Was it irreverent on the part of our forefathers to employ the same pronoun in praying to God as they used in daily speech one to another? If not, why should it be considered so now? We may find it difficult to accept the fact that Cranmer used contemporary language when he put together the English Prayer Book; but fact it is all the same.

In compiling *Parish Prayers* I found ample material from which to make my selection, for prayers in the older tradition are plentiful enough. It is by no means the same when it comes to prayers in modern idiom. Not many collections of any substance or quality have yet appeared, though I have gladly borrowed from a number of existing sources. Grateful acknowledgment of permission to use such prayers is made at the end of the volume. In particular I have drawn upon the Church Pastoral-Aid Society's *Prayers for Today's Church* (1972), edited by Dick Williams, and from the new edition of *New Every Morning* (1973) which I edited for the British Broadcasting Corporation. I wish to express my thanks to both the CPAS and BBC Publications for allowing me to reproduce material from these sources. I am also grateful to the authors of the prayers reprinted here for their co-operation in this matter. The names of all such are listed in the Acknowledgments.

A good many prayers have been written specially for this collection and now appear for the first time. In this respect I must thank the following for their contributions: the Rev. Michael Botting, the Rev. Llewellyn Cumings, the Rev. Christopher Idle, Canon Basil Naylor, and the Rev. Roger Pickering. In addition to these I am particularly indebted to Bishop George Appleton, the

Ven. Timothy Dudley-Smith, and the Rev. James M. Todd for so readily allowing me to make use of their prayers. Many others have also contributed prayers on a smaller scale.

If in any instance I have inadvertently ascribed prayers to wrong sources, or infringed any copyrights, I offer my apology to those concerned and will make amends in any subsequent editions. Where no ascription appears at the end of a prayer the source or authorship is unknown. In certain cases prayers have been altered or shortened for the purpose of this book, and where this has been done an asterisk (*) has been added to the ascription. Prayers described as *Adapted* have been derived from various sources, known and unknown, and in most cases have been considerably modified or rewritten by myself. As for my own prayers, which I am aware form an undue proportion of the whole, perhaps I should explain that they have been written over a fairly considerable period of time, some at the request of others, some for specific occasions, some expressly for the present work in an endeavour to fill gaps or provide additional material.

It remains for me to add a word of thanks to Mr. Edward England of Messrs. Hodder and Stoughton for his patience with me from the time I first discussed this project with him some three or four years ago. Now that the task is completed I express the hope, which I know he shares, that the book will prove serviceable to the prayer life of the Church at large.

FRANK COLQUHOUN

Norwich Cathedral,
January 1975

I
PRAYERS FOR THE CHURCH'S YEAR

ADVENT

The Coming of Christ 1

WE praise you, Lord Christ, that in your infinite love you came to save us from our sins and to bring us to God.

We praise you that you come to us now in the power of your Spirit to strengthen us for service and to abide with us all our days.

Help us to remember that you will come again in your majesty to be our judge, that we may dedicate our lives to the furtherance of your kingdom.

We ask it for the honour and glory of your name.

Frank Colquhoun

2

Make clear to us, O Lord our God,
  the meaning of Christ's coming
    to Bethlehem long ago,
    in our lives now,
    and at the last great day;
  that we may receive his forgiveness,
  know the power of his living presence,
  and rejoice in the hope of his kingdom;
  for his name's sake. *Roger Pickering*

3

O God of all hope, we thank you for all your promises which find their fulfilment in your Son. So we rejoice in his coming in the flesh and look for his appearing in glory. By your Word and Holy Spirit make us ready to receive Christ truly as our only Lord and Saviour, and with thankfulness to praise him, now and for ever.

4

O Lord our God, make us watchful and keep us faithful as we await the coming of your Son our Lord; that when he shall appear he may find us not sleeping in sin but active in his service and joyful in his praise, for the glory of your holy name.

Adapted from Gelasian collect

5

Grant, O God, that as we rejoice in the hope of the coming of our Saviour, we may seek to prepare the way of his coming by advancing his kingdom in the world and caring for the needs of our fellow men; through the same Jesus Christ our Lord.

Adapted

The judgment
6

O Lord Christ, before whose judgment seat we must all appear: keep us steadfast and faithful in your service; and enable us so to judge ourselves in this life, that we may not be condemned in the day of your appearing; for your tender mercy's sake.

Based on William Bright

7

Lord Jesus, Redeemer and Judge of men,
    who came to save us from our sins:
you have taught us that you will come again
    to take account of your servants
    and to reward faithful service.
Help us to live as men who wait for their master,
    with loins girded, alert and ready for action,
    with lamps burning, maintaining a good witness;
that we may not be ashamed before you at your coming
    but enter into your eternal joy.   *Frank Colquhoun*

The Bible 8

Father, we thank you for giving us the Bible as your written Word, the record of your revelation to mankind for all generations.

Guide us in our reading of it, that we may not only know its teaching but also understand its meaning; and may its message both be written in our hearts and be made manifest in our lives; for the glory of him who is the living Word, our Saviour Jesus Christ. *Frank Colquhoun*

9

Heavenly Father, give us the faith to receive your Word, the understanding to know what it means, and the courage to put it into practice; through Jesus Christ our Lord. *Alan Warren*

10

Lord God, whose Word and will are made known in Jesus Christ: inspire in us faith in that Word and obedience to that will, for our salvation and for your glory. *Worship Now*

11

O God, you have promised that your Word shall not fail of its purpose: we pray for all who this day will read or listen to some part of the Bible; that the Holy Spirit may open their eyes to see the truth, and their hearts to receive it; through Jesus Christ our Lord.

12

O God of truth, as you have given your Word to men, so strengthen the hands of all who have a part in making it more widely known in our day.

We pray for those engaged in the work of translation and production; for distributors and colporteurs; for teachers, pastors, and evangelists; that the timeless truth of the Bible may be communicated to men and speak to their needs in living language and with saving power; through Jesus Christ our Lord. *Adapted*

13

Enable us, our Father,
 to respond to the grace of your Word
with humility of heart
 and in the spirit of loving obedience;
that our wills may be brought into submission
 to your perfect will,
and our lives be conformed more and more
 to the image of your Son,
  Jesus Christ our Lord.

Stewardship of time   **14**

O God, teach us to view time in the light of eternity, and help us to remember that no one of us knows how many or how few days may be left to us. So keep us faithful to our stewardship, that when our Lord comes we may be found using wisely our time and talents, our life and strength, and may merit his own "Well done"; for the honour of his name. *Adapted*

Preparing for Christmas   **15**

We give you our thanks, O God our Father, for the gift of your Son Jesus Christ, whose coming to this world was proclaimed by prophets of old and who was born for us in lowliness and poverty at Bethlehem.

As we make ready once again to celebrate his birth, fill our hearts with your own joy and peace, and enable us to welcome him as our Saviour; so that when he comes again in his glory and majesty he may find in us a people prepared for himself; who lives and reigns with you and the Holy Spirit, one God, now and for ever. *Frank Colquhoun*

16

O God our Father, we are preparing to celebrate the birthday of your Son Jesus Christ. While we recall his coming as a tiny baby in weakness and humility, may we be reminded that one day he will come in power and glory.

We make this prayer to you through the same Jesus Christ your Son, who lives and reigns with you in the unity of the Holy Spirit, for ever and ever. *Catholic Prayer Book*

17

Loving Father,
we thank you for the gift of your Son,
whose birth at Bethlehem
we now prepare to celebrate.
May our hearts and our homes
always be open to him,
that he may dwell with us for ever,
and we may serve him gladly all our days,
to the honour and glory of your name.

Roger Pickering

18

Our heavenly Father, as once again we prepare for Christmas, help us to find time in our busy lives for quiet and thought and prayer; that we may reflect upon the wonder of your love and allow the story of the Saviour's birth to penetrate our hearts and minds. So may our joy be deeper, our worship more real, and our lives worthier of all that you have done for us through the coming of your Son, Jesus Christ our Lord. *Frank Colquhoun*

CHRISTMAS

Adoration and thanksgiving 19

GLORY be to God for the wonder of his love made known to us in the birth of our Saviour Jesus Christ.

Glory be to God for the gift of his Son, who took our flesh of the Virgin Mary his mother and shared our human life.

Glory be to God for the great salvation he has sent to us and to all mankind, bringing joy to the world.

For these manifold blessings and for all the wonder of Christmas, glory be to God for ever and ever.   *Frank Colquhoun*

20

We bless and adore you, O Christ,
   Son of God, yet born of Mary;
   eternal Word, yet a child without speech;
   clothed in glory, yet wrapped in swaddling bands;
   Lord of heaven and earth, yet laid in a manger.

To you, O Jesus, strong in your weakness, glorious in your humility, mighty to save, be all praise and glory, with the Father and the Holy Spirit, now and for ever.   *Worship Now*★

21

We give thanks to the Father at this Christmas time
   for the gift of his Son to be our Saviour;
   for the love of Christ in taking our human nature;
   for his lowly birth at Bethlehem;
   and for the great redemption he has brought to us and to all
     mankind.
And with the angelic host we too would cry,

Glory to God in the highest,
and on earth peace, goodwill towards men!

Frank Colquhoun

The meaning of Christmas 22

Heavenly Father, we pray that amid all the joys and festivities of this season we may not forget what Christmas really means: that you loved the world so much that you gave your only Son, who was born to be our Saviour.

Accept our thanksgiving, and fill us with the spirit of charity and goodwill, that we may show our gratitude in generous service to those who need our help; for Jesus Christ's sake.

Frank Colquhoun

23

O God our Father, we ask that your Son's birth as a little child may deliver us from the old slavery that holds us fast beneath the yoke of sin.

Lord Jesus, by the example you gave in the poverty of your birth, teach us not to become so engrossed in material things that we lose sense of the true values of life.

Spirit of love, inspire us with generosity towards people in misfortune and distress.

We ask these prayers, giving glory to God in the highest, now and for evermore. *Catholic Prayer Book*★

God has spoken 24

We thank you, Lord God, for your word
spoken of old through prophets and apostles
and recorded for us in holy scripture;
and most of all for your final Word
spoken to us in your Son Jesus Christ,
made flesh for us men and for our salvation.
Grant that through the written word

we may behold the glory of the incarnate Word,
who is now exalted to the right hand of the Majesty on high,
and to whom we ascribe all praise and dominion
for ever and ever.   *Based on Hebrews 1. 1–3*

Good news   25

We praise you, Lord God, for the good news of Christmas:
    for the coming of your Son to redeem mankind.
Let it be good news for each one of us at this time
    as we open our hearts to your love
    and welcome Jesus as our Saviour.
Then show us what we can do
    to pass on the good news to others,
that they may share our joy
    and give thanks with us for your unspeakable gift
    in Jesus Christ our Lord.   *Frank Colquhoun*

26

God of love, open the hearts and minds of many this Christmas
time to the good and saving news of Jesus Christ; that those whose
lives are insecure, or empty, or aimless, may find in the one born
at Bethlehem all that they need today, and much more besides.
For his name's sake.   *Christopher Idle★*

Christmas peace   27

O God, we thank you for the message of peace that Christmas
brings to our distracted world. Give peace among the nations;
peace in our land; peace in our homes, and peace in our hearts, as
we remember the birth at Bethlehem of the Prince of Peace,
Jesus Christ our Lord.   *Worship Now*

28

Sweet Child of Bethlehem, grant that we may share with all
our hearts in this profound mystery of Christmas.

Pour into the hearts of men the peace which they sometimes seek so desperately and which you alone can give them.

Help them to know one another better and to live as brothers, children of the same Father.

Awaken in their hearts love and gratitude for your infinite goodness; join them together in your love; and give us all your heavenly peace.   *Pope John XXIII*

Christmas giving   29

O God, giver of all good gifts, at this time of the giving and receiving of gifts, help us to remember that Jesus said, "It is more blessed to give than to receive." And put into our hearts that love which knows that true happiness comes from making others happy, and true wealth from sharing all we have; through Jesus Christ our Lord.   *William Barclay*

A family prayer   30

Jesus, child of Mary, born into a human family,
the sharer of our human lot,
be with us in our homes this Christmas time.
Bless our children, our families and our friends.
Fill us with joy and thanksgiving;
Deepen our sense of wonder
as we understand more of your great love;
and teach us to find our true happiness
in giving rather than in receiving.
We ask it for the honour of your name.

Frank Colquhoun

The Bethlehem shepherds   31

We recall at this time how the shepherds, having heard the good news of the Saviour's birth, hastened to Bethlehem and found the babe lying in a manger, and how they glorified God for all that they had heard and seen.

Our Father, we pray that we too,
  as we listen again to the Christmas story,
may journey in thought to Bethlehem
  and bow in wonder and worship before the child in the
    manger,
  the Word made flesh,
and ascribe all honour, glory and praise to you,
  the God of our salvation,
now and for ever. *Frank Colquhoun*

The homeless at Christmas **32**

Son of Man, our friend and brother,
  you were born in a stable
  because there was no room in the inn.
While we celebrate your birthday
  in the comfort of our homes this Christmas
we remember those who have no homes
  and all who live in sordid dwellings.
Give us understanding of their need.
Show us what we can do to help.
And make us generous in our love and gifts
  because of Bethlehem,
  because of your love for us all. *Frank Colquhoun*

33

Save us, O God, from the hypocrisy of enjoying our Christmas in comfort and luxury while we do nothing to help the homeless families in our land and the refugees of other countries.

Fill our hearts with the love that cares and understands and gives, and show us how best we can serve those in need, for the sake of him who was born in a stable and laid in a manger, Jesus Christ our Lord. *Frank Colquhoun*

34

Lord Jesus Christ, born in a stable, hear the cry of the homeless and refugees; and so move our wills by your Holy Spirit that we may not rest content until all have found home and livelihood, for your name's sake.　　　　　　　　*New Every Morning*

Serving others　　　　　　　　**35**

Father, we pray that the joy of Christmas may fill our hearts with a new and deeper sense of your love for us and for your world, and that we may reflect your love by serving those in need; for his sake who came to be the Saviour of us all, Jesus Christ our Lord.　　　　　　　　*After William Bright*

Before a Christmas carol service　　　　　　　　**36**

Lord Jesus, when you came to this earth as a little child and lay in the manger at Bethlehem, the angels sang for joy and proclaimed glory to God in the highest.

As we now celebrate your birth these hundreds of years later we too would sing and be glad.

Accept our worship, the praises of our lips and the thanksgiving of our hearts, and bring us at last to your eternal joy, where you live and reign in the glory of the Father and the Holy Spirit, one God, now and for ever.　　　　　　　　*Frank Colquhoun*

37

The angels sang when Christ was born,
　　and so must we.
With thankful hearts we celebrate his nativity
　　and lift up our voices in joyful song;
with the heavenly host we cry,
　　Glory to God in the highest!
Accept, O Lord God, our worship;
　　and as we hear again the Christmas story
　　in word and song

show us something more of your great love
in Jesus Christ your Son our Lord.

Frank Colquhoun

38

Lord, we've sung these carols and heard this story so many times before.

We confess that we have allowed the most important event in history to become dulled by familiarity.

Help us in this act of worship to recapture a sense of wonder.

Let us discover with surprise the stupendous fact that the Creator of the universe has shown himself in a newborn baby.

Enable us to accept what we shall never fully understand.

So may our worship be filled with spontaneous joy.

J. D. Searle

The Blessing **39**

Go in peace:
the wisdom of the Wonderful Counsellor guide you,
the strength of the Mighty God defend you,
the love of the Everlasting Father enfold you,
the peace of the Prince of Peace be upon you.
And the blessing of God Almighty,
Father, Son, and Holy Spirit
be upon you all this night and for evermore.

Worship Now

NEW YEAR

Thanksgiving and prayer   **40**

WE give thanks, our heavenly Father, for the goodness and
mercy which have followed us all the days of our life, and
especially through the year that is now past; and we pray that in
the year ahead your wisdom may direct us, your power defend
us, and your love enfold us; through Jesus Christ our Lord.

Frank Colquhoun

41

Heavenly Father, whose mercy is everlasting,
   accept our thanksgiving for all the blessing of the year that is
      past;
   take our lives afresh into your keeping as we face the unknown
      future;
   and fit us by your grace for whatever lies before us in the days
      to come;
for the sake of your Son our Saviour Jesus Christ.

Frank Colquhoun

The unchanging Lord   **42**

Grant, Lord, that as the years change
   we may find rest in your eternal changelessness.
May we go forward into this year with courage,
   sure in the faith that while life changes around us
you are always the same,
   guiding us with your wisdom
   and protecting us with your love.
So may the peace which passes all understanding
   keep our hearts and minds in Christ Jesus our Lord.

Harold E. Evans

43

Eternal Lord God, the same yesterday, today, and for ever: as we begin this new year we ask your help in forgetting the mistakes of the past, in facing the problems and challenges of the present, and in renewing our sense of hope for the future, as we go forward in the name of Jesus Christ our Lord.   *Response**

The possibilities ahead   **44**

For all the possibilities ahead in this new year,
make us thankful, O Lord.
Give us wisdom, courage, and discernment
in the face of so much chaos, despair, and fear.
Help us to see how, in our circumstances,
we can contribute towards peace, faith, and love.
And give us the will to translate our desires into actions.
Brother John Charles, SSF

The Circumcision of Christ   **45**

Lord Jesus, circumcised for us on the eighth day, and given the name Jesus according to the word of the angel: fulfil to us the gracious promise of that name, and keep us ever joyful in your salvation, to the glory of God the Father.   *Adapted*

Dedication   **46**

All through this year, O Father,
help us to know Christ better
and to make him better known,
by yielding our wills to his lordship
and our lives to the service of others;
for Jesus Christ's sake.   *Maurice A. P. Wood*

EPIPHANY

An act of praise **47**

ALMIGHTY and everlasting God, who by the guidance of a star led the magi from eastern lands to adore the new-born King:
we praise you for giving your Son Jesus Christ to be the light of the world, and for revealing in him your saving love to all mankind.

We praise you for the light of the everlasting gospel sent forth to every nation and race, and shining so long among us.

We praise you for your Church universal, the whole company of Christ's people, worshipping him and bearing witness to him in every land.

Receive, O Lord, these our praises, and fill the world with the radiance of your glory, that all men may come and render homage to Christ, their Saviour and their King.

Adapted from various sources

The magi **48**

Lord God, we remember how you led the wise men to Bethlehem by the light of a star. Guide us as we travel to the heavenly city, that we and all men may know Jesus as the true and living way, for his name's sake. *Family Worship*

49

O God our Father, who by the bright shining of a star
led the wise men to the city of David:
guide us by the light of your Spirit,
that we too may come into the presence of Jesus
and offer our gifts and our worship to him,
our Saviour and our Lord. *Alan Warren*

50

Almighty God, whose glory the heavens are telling, we pray that as you led the wise men by the light of a star to your infant Son, to worship in him the Word made flesh, so by the light of the gospel you will guide the nations of the earth into the way of truth, that the whole world may be filled with your glory; through Jesus Christ our Lord. *Adapted*

Our Bethlehem 51

O God, we need a star to set our journey through the world. Help us to see in the babe born at Bethlehem the eternal star which will lead us to the place where truth and love and mercy meet, so that we may kneel with shepherds and kings and find heart's joy and heart's peace in Jesus Christ. *George Appleton*

Dedication 52

Our Father, as we remember at this time the story of the wise men and the gifts they brought to the infant King, we pray that we in our turn may offer him the gold of obedience, the incense of lowliness, and the myrrh of devotion; and all for his honour and praise. *Adapted*

53

Heavenly Father, whose kingdom rules over all,
we pray that as the wise men from distant lands
brought their gifts to the Christ child
and paid him homage,
so we may offer our lives to him
and rejoice to own him as our King,
for the glory of his great name. *Adapted*

The light of Christ 54

We praise you, O God, that the light of Christ shines amid the darkness of our world, and that the darkness has not overcome it;

and we pray that his light may shine more and more into our own lives, illuminating our minds with the knowledge of the truth and enabling us to walk in the way of holiness and love; through the same Jesus Christ our Lord. *Frank Colquhoun*

55

O God, who in the work of creation
    commanded the light to shine out of darkness:
we pray that the light of the glorious gospel of Christ
    may shine into the hearts of men everywhere,
dispelling the darkness of their ignorance and unbelief
    and revealing to them the knowledge of your glory
    in the face of Jesus Christ our Lord.

Based on 2 Corinthians 4. 4–6

56

Lord God, whose Son Jesus Christ was manifested amid the darkness of the world as the light of life: we pray that his light may so shine among the nations that all peoples may come to know him, worship him, and serve him; to whom be glory now and for evermore. *Frank Colquhoun*

The baptism of Jesus

57

Almighty God, who proclaimed Jesus to be your beloved Son when the Holy Spirit came down upon him at his baptism in the Jordan, grant that we who have been baptized in his name may rejoice in being your sons and the servants of all, through Jesus Christ our Lord *A Christian's Prayer Book*

58

Heavenly Father, who sent the Holy Spirit on your Son at his baptism to anoint him for the service of mankind: send your Spirit now to us who have been made your children by adoption and grace, that we may follow in his steps and work for the coming of his kingdom, to the glory of his name. *Adapted*

The first sign   **59**

Almighty God, the giver of strength and joy, whose Son turned the water into wine at Cana in Galilee: change our bondage into liberty, and the poverty of our nature into the riches of your grace; that by the transformation of our lives your glory may be revealed; through Jesus Christ our Lord.

*Book of Common Worship**

LENT

ALMIGHTY God, we pray that through this season of Lent, by prayer and study and self-discipline, we may penetrate more deeply into the mystery of Christ's sufferings; that following in the way of his cross and passion we may come to share in the glory and triumph of his resurrection; through the same Jesus Christ our Lord. *Adapted*

61

Lord Christ, who came to call
   not the righteous but sinners to repentance:
help us in this season of Lent
   to hear and respond to your call;
that by your grace we may turn from whatever in our lives
   is at variance with your will,
and walk in the way of holiness and love,
   to the glory of God the Father. *Frank Colquhoun*

62

Teach us, O God, so to use this season of Lent
   that we may be drawn closer to our Lord,
and in fellowship with him may learn
   to hate sin,
   to overcome temptation,
   and to grow in holiness,
that our lives may be strengthened for your service
   and used for your glory.
We ask this in Christ's name. *Frank Colquhoun*

63

Holy Father, whose Son Jesus Christ fasted forty days in the desert, give us grace to discipline ourselves in humble submission to your Spirit, that we may lead upright and holy lives to your honour and glory; through the same Jesus Christ our Lord.

A Christian's Prayer Book

64

Help us this Lent, O Lord, to know ourselves better, and give us strength to root out of our lives the unsuspected sins and the weak spots in our characters.

Help us this Lent, O Lord, to cultivate self-mastery, and give us self-control where we are most likely to succumb to temptation.

Help us this Lent, O Lord, to practise self-denial, that we may be more ready to give of our time, our energy, and our leisure in service to others.

So may we come to the joyful season of Easter stronger and more faithful disciples of our Lord and Master Jesus Christ.

Prayers at School★

For use in Lent **65**

Heavenly Father, as we remember at this time the temptations and sufferings of our Lord, we pray for grace to follow him in the way of self-denial.

Give us true penitence and sorrow for sin.

Help us to renounce the world and to put to death the deeds of the flesh.

And strengthen us so to overcome temptation in the power of the Holy Spirit, that in all things we may be more than conquerors through our Saviour Jesus Christ. *Frank Colquhoun*

66

Heavenly Father, give us more charity, more self-denial, more likeness to Christ. Teach us that it is better to give than to receive; better to forget ourselves than to put ourselves forward; better to serve than to be served, after the example of your Son, Jesus Christ our Lord. *Henry Alford**

67

By the prayers of Jesus,
  Lord, teach us how to pray.
By the gifts of Jesus,
  Lord, teach us how to give.
By the toils of Jesus,
  Lord, teach us how to work.
By the love of Jesus,
  Lord, teach us how to love.
By the cross of Jesus,
  Lord, teach us how to live.

Lent: springtime in the soul 68

Lord God, with Lent we approach the springtime of the year when the face of the earth is renewed and life emerges out of death.

We pray that this season of Lent may be a veritable springtime for our souls, so that our lives, quickened by the breath of the Spirit and warmed by the sunshine of your love, may bear abundant fruit and be made radiant with the beauty of holiness; through Jesus Christ our Lord. *Frank Colquhoun*

Penitence 69

O God, the searcher of hearts, help us to see ourselves in the light of your holiness, that we may hate and turn from our sins, receive your grace and forgiveness, and learn to love and serve you better; through Jesus Christ our Lord. *Frank Colquhoun*

70

Most merciful God and Father,
give us true repentance for our sins.
Open our eyes to recognize the truth about ourselves;
so that acknowledging our faults,
our weaknesses and our failures,
we may receive your forgiveness
and find in your love the encouragement
to make a new beginning;
for the sake of Jesus Christ our Lord.   *Response*

Temptation   71

Lord Jesus, we turn with confidence to you, knowing that you were tempted in all respects as we are, yet without sin.

Give us your help, that we may obtain victory over our temptations.

We are ashamed that we have so little power in our lives and that we so often fall at the same old hurdles. . . .

Teach us to remember the promise that those who wait upon the Lord shall renew their strength. May we wait and be made strong.

We ask it in your name and for your sake.

Based on a prayer of Peter Marshall

Reality in religion   72

God our Father, as those who profess and call ourselves Christians we ask you to save us from the sort of hypocrisy which our Lord Jesus condemned in the Pharisees of old.

Save us from a religion which is all on the outside; from paying you lip-service while our hearts are far from you.

Give us reality in our worship; teach us how to pray aright; and kindle in our hearts the spirit of true penitence, living faith, and love unfeigned.

We ask it all in Christ's name.   *Frank Colquhoun*

God of truth, save us from a religion of mere words:
    from repeating pious phrases which have lost their meaning;
    from uttering empty prayers which have no soul;
    from calling Jesus "Lord, Lord", when we fail to own his
       sovereignty.
We pray that the gospel may come into our lives
    not in word only but also in the power of the Spirit,
and that our love may not be a matter of words or talk
    but be genuine and show itself in action.
Help us, our Father, to mean this our prayer
    as we ask it in the name of Christ our Lord.

Frank Colquhoun

MOTHERING SUNDAY

Thanksgiving **74**

LORD Jesus, who came to share our life here on earth and made
your home among us at Nazareth: we thank you for our
homes and families, and especially today for our mothers and
for all that they mean to us.

Bless them, O Lord, and bless our homes; and help us to find
our true happiness in loving and serving one another for your
sake, our Master and our Friend. *Frank Colquhoun*

For mothers **75**

        Lord Jesus, you know well
        the blessings an earthly home can bring:
        receive our thanks for all the love
        we have enjoyed in our homes,
        especially from those who have nurtured us
        from our earliest years;
        and hear our prayer for mothers everywhere,
        that they may never lose heart,

> nor ever be taken for granted,
> but may, with Mary your mother,
> receive the honour they deserve.
> O Lord Jesus, bless them and keep them,
> now and for ever. *Roger Pickering*

God's family 76

Heavenly Father, we thank you for making us in our baptism members of your worldwide family the Church, and for our brothers and sisters in every land who love the Lord Jesus. Keep us loyal to one another, faithful to our promises, and busy in your service, for Jesus Christ's sake. *Frank Colquhoun*

A prayer to be said by all 77

> Heavenly Father, whose love enfolds us all,
> may your kingdom come
> within my heart,
> within our homes,
> through all our land,
> and in all the world,
> for Jesus' sake.
> *Church Teaching for the Junior Child* ★

PASSIONTIDE

78

G OD our Father, in obedience to whose will
   our Saviour Christ became man
and suffered on the cross for our redemption:
help us by your grace to learn from his meekness
    and to partake of the benefits of his passion,
that we may share his triumph
    and know the joy of his resurrection;
who now lives and reigns with you and the Holy Spirit
    for ever and ever. *Frank Colquhoun*

79

O God, the Father of all mankind, who loved the world so
much that you gave your only Son to die for man's salvation:
make us, who have been redeemed by his precious blood, to die
with him to sin, to rise with him to righteousness, and to walk
with him in newness of life; through the merits of the same Jesus
Christ our Lord. *Adapted*

80

Almighty and everlasting God,
    whose Son our Saviour Jesus Christ
triumphed in death on the cross
    that he might win life for the world:
help us in the power of his victory
    to triumph over all evil
    and to glory in his cross alone;
who is alive and reigns with you and the Holy Spirit,
    one God for ever and ever. *James M. Todd*

Life through death   81

Lord Christ, you have reminded us that a grain of wheat remains a single grain unless it falls into the ground and dies, but that if it dies it bears a rich harvest.

Grant that we, like the grain of wheat, may die to self, so that we may live for others and follow you in the path of sacrifice and service, to the glory of God the Father.   *Basil Naylor*

Based on John 12. 24–6

Palm Sunday   82

Lord, on this Palm Sunday you were given a hero's welcome as one who was going the way of the crowd; but you had chosen the way of the cross, and the applause was short lived.

Keep bright and clear before us the vision of our calling, that we may never be diverted from the way you have chosen for us, but may follow in the steps of you, our crucified and risen Lord, to whom be all glory, laud and honour, this day and for evermore.

Basil Naylor

83

Lord God in majesty,
true King of heaven and earth,
it is in men's hearts that you wish to reign.
Help us to give ourselves without reserve
to the one who entered Jerusalem on a donkey
and received a crown of thorns;
for he is now seated with you in glory,
to reign with you to the end of time.

Roger Pickering

84

Lord Jesus, you showed the world your princely power by riding into Jerusalem on a donkey: help us to understand the humility of your journey to the cross, so that we may experience

the glory of your victory over sin and death. We ask it for your
name's sake. *Alan Warren*

He emptied himself 85

> We worship you, O Christ, because for our sake
>   you laid aside your power and glory
> and clothed yourself in the garment of our humanity,
>   to live in poverty here on earth
>   and to suffer death upon the cross.
> Teach us the lesson of your humility,
>   and empty our lives of all pride and selfishness,
> that we may find our joy and fulfilment
>   in serving others in your name and for your sake.
>   *Frank Colquhoun*

Holy Week 86

> Father in heaven, as your people prepare once more
> to follow the events of Good Friday and Easter,
> may we be led by your Spirit to deeper insights
> into your love and saving grace;
> that we may love you more and serve you better,
> for the sake of him who died for us and rose again,
> our Lord and Saviour Jesus Christ.   *Roger Pickering*

87

Lord Jesus Christ, betrayed for thirty pieces of silver, deserted
by your disciples, denied by Peter, mocked by Herod, scourged
by Pilate, crowned with thorns, and nailed to the cross: humbly
and with all our heart we thank you for your suffering and death,
by which we have been forgiven and redeemed.

J. W. G. Masterton

88

Most merciful God, Redeemer of all mankind,
  give us such a vision of the cross of Calvary
that we may turn to you with true and deep repentance,
  acknowledging our unworthiness,
  pouring contempt on all our pride,
  and offering our lives back to you;
that in service of your kingdom we may show our gratitude
  for all that you have done for us
  in Jesus Christ our Lord. *Adapted*

The cleansing of the temple 89

O God most holy, whose Son our Lord Jesus Christ cast out
from the temple those who desecrated the holy place: cleanse
your Church from all falsehood and hypocrisy, from dissension
and all uncharitableness, that it may become a house of prayer for
all nations, to the glory of your name. *Frank Colquhoun*

90

Lord Jesus Christ, who in the week of your passion cleansed the
temple in Jerusalem: purify our hearts from all defilement, our
worship from all insincerity, and our lives from all selfishness;
that we may become a holy temple in the Lord, a dwelling place
for God in the Spirit. *Adapted*

The Lord's Supper 91

Lord Christ, we recall at this time how on that solemn passover
night you met with your disciples in the upper room and hallowed bread and wine as the memorials of your body and blood.

We thank you for this sacrament of our redemption and for
all that it reveals to us of your love; and we pray that whenever
we meet at your table to obey your command, "Do this in remembrance of me", we may know your risen presence in our
midst and feed upon you, the true Bread from heaven, till we
come to your everlasting kingdom. *Frank Colquhoun*

92

Lord Jesus, in the sacrament of your body and blood
you have graciously given us a way to remember
both your sacrifice for us
and your presence with us.
May we receive your salvation in its fullness
and give ourselves gladly in the service of others,
that all may be drawn into your glorious kingdom,
to the praise of your great name. *Roger Pickering*

See also prayers for Holy Communion, 586–99

The feet washing

93

Jesus Lord and Master, who served your disciples in washing
their feet: serve us often, serve us daily, in washing our motives,
our ambitions, our actions; that we may share with you in your
mission to the world and serve others gladly for your sake; to
whom be glory for ever. *Based on The Christian Priest Today,*
by Michael Ramsey

94

Son of Man, who on the night before your passion took towel
and water and washed the feet of your disciples: give us understanding of what you have done, and teach us to follow the
example of your humility, that by love we may serve one another
for love of you, our Saviour and our Lord. *Frank Colquhoun*

GOOD FRIDAY

The day of the cross **95**

LORD Jesus, on this Good Friday we remember with penitence and gratitude the agony and shame, the darkness and desolation, you endured on Calvary for us and for the redemption of mankind.

As we meet under the shadow of the cross we ask you to help us to understand something more of what it cost you, the Holy One, to bear away our sin, that we may love and serve you better, our only Mediator and most merciful Redeemer, to whom be glory for ever and ever. *Frank Colquhoun*

96

O God, whose Son Jesus Christ, for the redemption of the world, consented to be betrayed, rejected, denied, and forsaken; to be accused, condemned, scourged, spat upon, and crowned with thorns; to hang in agony on the cross, to bear the weight of the world's sin, to die and to be buried in the grave: help us at this time to remember that it was for us men and for our salvation he suffered these things, and most thankfully to receive the benefits of his passion; who is now alive and reigns with you and the Holy Spirit, one God, for ever and ever. *After William Bright*

97

Lord Christ, as we draw near to you this day
under the shadow of the cross,
give us a new understanding of your sorrow over us,
true repentance for our sins for which you suffered,
and an ever deeper gratitude for your redeeming love
for us and for all mankind.

98

O God, we are not worthy of this your greatest gift, that Christ shed his blood for us. Forgive us that we are so slow to respond and to show the gratitude we owe in faithful service and loving deed; and help us as we hear the story of the cross once again to become alive to what it meant to him, and what it involves for us. *Roger Tomes*

In debt to Christ 99

Lord Jesus, we praise you for your redeeming love
  and all that you have done for us.
As we bow in penitence before the cross
  we gratefully acknowledge the debt we owe.
For ours was the sin you bore,
  ours the ransom you paid,
  ours the salvation you won.
Lord Jesus, accept our thanksgiving
  and make us more worthy of your love;
    for your love's sake. *Frank Colquhoun*

The rent veil 100

Father, we thank you that on the first Good Friday
  the veil of the temple was torn in two
    from the top to the bottom.
And so we thank you that through Christ's passion
  and his full and perfect sacrifice for sin
the way to your presence is now open
  to us and to all men.
Accept our thanksgiving, and teach us to draw near
  with a true heart in full assurance of faith
as we tread that new and living way,
  through him who is our great high priest,
    your Son Jesus Christ our Lord. *Frank Colquhoun*
      Based on Hebrews 10. 19–22

THE SEVEN WORDS FROM THE CROSS

Introduction   101

LORD Jesus Christ, in all your words most wonderful: assist us
by your Spirit as we now reflect again upon your last words
spoken from the cross.

Fill them with fresh meaning for each one of us here.

Help us to hear them with understanding,

to receive them with penitence,

and to respond to them with faith;

that we may grasp something more of the breadth and length,

the height and depth of your love which surpasses knowledge.

We ask this for your love's sake.   *Frank Colquhoun*

The first word "Father, forgive them"   102

It was your love, Lord Jesus,

that caused you to be nailed to the cross.

It was your love that held you there

when you might have called for legions of angels.

It was your love that pleaded for your murderers

and prayed "Father, forgive them".

Help us, most gracious Lord,

to grasp something more of your love,

to receive your forgiveness,

and to learn to forgive others

even as we have been forgiven,

for your love's sake.   *Frank Colquhoun*

103

Give us the power, Lord Jesus,

to forgive even at the moment

when suffering and shock are greatest.

Though our eyes sting and blur with pain,

help our hearts to grasp that those who hurt us

are so often unaware of what they do,
and to remember that in our sufferings
you, O Lord, are made to suffer too. *Roger Pickering*

104

Sinless Lord, you prayed for the forgiveness of those who
drove nails into your hands and feet:

help us sinners to grasp the immensity of your love and the
triviality of the wrongs inflicted on us, and to forgive as you did.
For your sake. *Michael Botting*

The second word "With me in paradise" **105**

O Christ, the King of glory,
   when you had vanquished the sting of death
you opened the kingdom of heaven
   to all who believe in you.
Accept our praise for your surpassing love
   in dying for sinful men.
Open your kingdom to us
   as you did to the penitent thief;
and remember us now, O Lord,
   and in the hour of our death,
for your great mercy's sake. *Frank Colquhoun*

106

In all the experiences of life,
deserved and undeserved,
and in the mystery of death,
O Lord Jesus,
may we have you at our side,
and may your promise sustain us
through the darkest hour. *Roger Pickering*

47

Merciful Lord, you promised paradise to a penitent thief:
help us sinners to grasp the reality of your love and forgiveness
to those who repent, and to share the message of your mercy
with those who think life is hopeless. For your sake.

Michael Botting

The third word "Behold your son! Behold your mother!"

We thank you, Lord Christ,
   that by the travail of your passion
you brought to birth the new redeemed family of the Church,
   in which your love transfigures all our relationships.
Draw us as believers closer together
   at the foot of the cross.
Teach us to welcome and care for one another
   in obedience to your word;
and unite us in a fellowship of compassion
   as members of the one family,
to serve our Father's kingdom and to do his will,
   to the glory of his name.

Frank Colquhoun

Lord, as we stand at the cross with Mary
and hear your words,
   still caring even in your agony,
   we ask you to work in us your desire;
   that as humble members of your family
   we may care deeply for each other,
   and unselfishly commend your love
   in word and deed.

Roger Pickering

110

Compassionate Lord, you made provision for your mother when others provided nothing but pain and suffering for you:

help us sinners to forget our own troubles and to dedicate ourselves to the relief of others. For your sake.

Michael Botting

The fourth word "Forsaken me?"   **111**

> Out of the darkness of Calvary,
>   O holy Son of God,
> we hear your lonely cry of dereliction,
>   and we bow in penitence,
>   we acknowledge our guilt.
> You bore our sins in your body on the tree.
>   You were made a curse for us;
>   you tasted death for every man.
> Jesus, Lamb of God, Saviour of the world,
>   have mercy upon us,
> and teach us to know that you were forsaken
>   that we might never be forsaken
> but walk in the light of God's presence,
>   now and for evermore.   *Frank Colquhoun*

112

> Father in heaven,
> we wonder how you must have felt
> when you heard your Son's cry,
> "Why have you abandoned me?"
> Spare us from such depths of dereliction;
> but if it be necessary for us
> to touch even the edges of it,
> keep us in the knowledge
> that for our Lord Jesus
> it was not the end.   *Roger Pickering*

49

Long-suffering Lord, you bore the dereliction of hell that we might know the rapture of heaven:

help us sinners to spare no effort to bring the good news of your sacrifice to a world otherwise without hope. For your sake.

Michael Botting

The fifth word "I am thirsty" 114

Son of Man, who endured in your body
 the agony of thirst in death,
and in your spirit thirsted
 for the world's salvation:
deepen our understanding of your sufferings
 by which our redemption was secured,
and increase in us those spiritual longings
 which you alone can satisfy;
that hungering and thirsting after righteousness
 we may be filled with all the fullness of God
 and serve and praise you evermore.

Frank Colquhoun

115

Teach us, O God,
 never to be above asking for help,
 nor reluctant to give it;
for in the simplest request
 we affirm our manhood,
and by the smallest kindness
 may be serving our Lord,
who having suffered now offers us
 the living water of eternal life.

Roger Pickering

116

Suffering Lord, you thirsted for us on the cross that the longings of our souls might be satisfied:

help us sinners to thirst after you and your righteousness, that your passion may not have been in vain. For your sake.

Michael Botting

The sixth word "Finished!"   **117**

O Saviour of the world, we praise you again
    for the victory of the cross
    and for your finished work.
You have done for us
    what we could never do for ourselves,
and what we did not deserve you to do;
    and you have done it once and for all.
Through your perfect and all-sufficient sacrifice
    sin is conquered,
    death is destroyed,
    man is redeemed,
    and heaven is opened.
To God be the glory for ever and ever.

Frank Colquhoun

118

We thank you, Lord Jesus,
for finishing the work you came to do;
for you came not only to teach
and to heal,
but to save from sin all who trust you.
We need you, Lord,
and we trust you,
for you are our hope and our God,
now and to the end of time.   *Roger Pickering*

119

Victorious Lord, you accomplished on the cross our complete redemption:

help us sinners not only to receive your salvation but to work out its consequences in our daily lives with awe and reverence, knowing that it will be completed when you return in triumph on the last day. For your sake.   *Michael Botting*

The seventh word "Into your hands . . ."   **120**

    Father of mercies and God of love,
      in his last word from the cross
    your Son our Saviour committed his spirit
      into your hands.
    We today would do the same.
    In your hands alone we are secure:
      there is no other place where we would be.
    And so, our Father, receive us now,
    as into your hands we commit ourselves,
      our souls and bodies,
      in life and in death,
        for time and for eternity.   *Frank Colquhoun*

121

    And now, O Father in heaven,
    we entrust ourselves to you;
    that living or dying,
    joyful or suffering,
    we may ever be with our Lord Jesus,
      safe in your eternal care.   *Roger Pickering*

122

Eternal Lord, your death on the cross has opened up for us a new and living way into the heavenly sanctuary:

help us sinners to commit our lives into your hands and to face death with your confidence. For your sake.   *Michael Botting*

EASTER

ETERNAL God and Father, by whose power
   our Lord Jesus Christ was raised from the dead:
with the whole company of your people
   in heaven and on earth
we rejoice and give thanks,
   that he who was dead is alive again
   and lives for evermore;
that he is with us now and always,
   and that nothing can part us from your love in him;
that he has opened the way to your kingdom
   and brought us the gift of eternal life.
All glory, praise and thanksgiving,
   all worship, honour and love,
be yours, almighty and everlasting God,
   in time and for all eternity.   *James M. Todd*

124

Christ is alive, the conqueror of all his foes, and ours.
Christ is alive, and in his hands are the keys of
   death and the unseen world.
Christ is alive, and in him we are born again to a
   living hope and an eternal inheritance.
We praise you, O Christ, for your resurrection victory.
We acknowledge you as our living Saviour and Lord.
We rejoice in hope of the glory of God.
Alleluia!   *Frank Colquhoun*

125

We give thanks, O God our Father, for the glorious resurrection of your Son our Lord from the dead:
for his victory over sin and the grave;
for his risen presence in our daily lives;
for his promise of life immortal with him.
Accept our praise, and teach us day by day to live rejoicingly in the faith of him who died for us, and rose again, and is alive for evermore, our Saviour Jesus Christ. *Frank Colquhoun*

126

God our Father, may the whole world join in a hymn of thanksgiving for the great love you have shown us in Jesus Christ our Lord, risen from the dead, and may our hearts and lives echo your praise, now and always. *A Christian's Prayer Book*★

127

Praise be to the God and Father of our Lord Jesus Christ!
In his great mercy he has given us new birth and a living hope
by raising Jesus Christ from the dead,
and the promise of a heavenly inheritance
which can never be spoilt or soiled or wither away.
Trusting in him we obtain the salvation of our souls
and rejoice with unutterable and exalted joy.
To him be glory now and for evermore.

Based on 1 Peter 1. 3–9

Easter joy   **128**

Almighty and everlasting God, we meet with joy
to worship you this Easter day.
And our joy is this,
that he who was crucified, dead and buried
is now alive for evermore,
our risen and reigning Lord.

As we celebrate his triumph
>we pray that his joy may abide in our hearts
>and that our lives may proclaim his praise.
To him be glory for ever and ever.   *Frank Colquhoun*

Easter hope   **129**

We worship you, our living, conquering Lord, because by your death you have broken the power of death, and by your glorious resurrection you have brought life and immortality to light.

As those who partake of your victory we pray that we may continually rejoice in this hope, and live on earth as those whose citizenship is in heaven, where you reign in the glory of the Father and the Holy Spirit for ever and ever.   *Frank Colquhoun*

130

Eternal God, in whom is all our hope
>in life, in death, and to all eternity:
grant that, rejoicing in the eternal life
>which is ours in Christ,
we may face whatever the future holds in store for us
>calm and unafraid,
always confident that neither death nor life
>can part us from your love in Jesus Christ our Lord.
>>>>*James M. Todd*

See also 627–8

Easter peace   **131**

Living Lord, conqueror of death, we remember with gladness how on the day of your resurrection you appeared to your disciples in your risen power and said to them, "Peace be with you".

Speak that word to our hearts today, O Lord.

Lift us above all our doubts and fears; and help us so to practise your presence and to rest upon your victory that your peace may be with us, now and for evermore.   *Frank Colquhoun*

Easter faith 132

    Lord our God, as we celebrate with joy
      the resurrection of Jesus our Saviour,
    help us to make the Easter faith
      a deeper reality in our lives;
    that we may know something more of the peace
      he bequeathed to his disciples,
    and lay hold of the victory
      he won for us over sin and death,
    rejoicing in the hope of the life immortal
      which is ours in him,
        our Redeemer and our Lord. *Frank Colquhoun*

Faith, hope and love 133

Lord, at this Easter time we ask you to increase our faith, our hope and our love.

Give us the faith that overcomes the world and enables us to face both life and death calm and unafraid.

Give us the hope that looks beyond this mortal life and grasps hold of the things unseen and eternal.

Give us the love that binds us more closely to one another, and to you our risen Lord; to whom be all glory and praise, dominion and power, now and for ever. *Adapted*

Risen with Christ 134

Help us, O Lord our God, to hear and obey your call to us, as those who have been raised with Christ, to seek the things that are above where Christ is, seated at your right hand; that our thoughts may be set on heavenly things, not on the things of earth, and we may be partakers of his risen life until we are manifested with him in glory. We ask it in his name.

Based on Colossians 3. 1–4

Our baptism 135

Almighty God, our heavenly Father, as we celebrate again the
rising of our Lord Jesus Christ from the grave, help us to remember that in our baptism we were united with him both in his
death and in his resurrection; that enabled by your grace we may
follow him in the way of holiness and be partakers of his victory,
to the honour and glory of your name.   *Adapted*

Mary Magdalene 136

Risen Lord Jesus, as Mary Magdalene met with you in the
garden on the morning of the resurrection, so may we meet with
you as we worship on this Easter day.
Speak to our hearts, as you spoke to her, by name.
Reveal yourself to us as the living Lord.
Renew our hope and rekindle our joy;
and commission us to go and share the good news with others.
We ask it in your name, to whom be glory for evermore.

Frank Colquhoun

Emmaus 137

Risen Lord, who on the first Easter day drew near to your two
disciples on the Emmaus road, and at evening stayed with them
in their village home: be our unseen companion along the daily
journey of our life, and at the ending of the day come and abide
with us in our dwellings; for your love's sake.

Frank Colquhoun

The great Shepherd 138

God of peace, whose Son our Lord Jesus was brought back
from the dead to become the great Shepherd of the sheep by the
blood that sealed an eternal covenant: equip us to do your will
in everything that is good, that our lives may always be acceptable
to you through Jesus Christ, to whom be glory for ever and ever.

Based on Hebrews 13. 20–1

The Lord's day 139

Lord Jesus Christ, by your resurrection from the dead you have hallowed the first day of the week as a day of worship for your people: may we so die to sin and rise to newness of life that we may be worthy to offer up our prayers and praises on this and every day, to the honour and glory of your name.

*Diocese of Melanesia**

Doxology 140

Lord Jesus Christ, you are the Lamb that was slain,
worthy to receive power and wisdom and might,
honour and glory and blessing,
now and for evermore. *Based on Revelation 5. 12*

The fruits of the earth **141**

ALMIGHTY God, by whose blessing the earth brings forth abundantly all that is needful for the life of man: prosper the work of farmers and those engaged in agriculture; that with thankful hearts they may reap the fruit of their labour, and we and all mankind may rejoice in your great goodness; through Jesus Christ our Lord. *New Every Morning*

142

Heavenly Father, as you have taught us to pray for our daily bread and to recognize our dependence on your bounty, so we ask your blessing on the sowing of the seed and the labours of those who work on the land; that the earth may yield its full harvest and the needs of all men may be supplied; through Jesus Christ our Lord. *Frank Colquhoun*

143

Heavenly Father, you have graciously given us
this world to live in:
may we respect both natural law
and the law of the Spirit;
that in using and sharing this world's resources
we may be made fit for the company of heaven;
through Jesus Christ our Lord. *Roger Pickering*

144

O God, from whom all good things do come,
make us unfeignedly thankful

for all the blessings of this life;
and give us both the wisdom and the will
to make your bounty available
to all who live on our earth,
that all may rejoice in your mercy;
through Jesus Christ our Lord. *Adapted*

A Rogation collect 145

Loving Father, you promise to supply all our needs
out of your abundant store:
prosper the labours of those who enable us
to enjoy the resources of nature,
whether by farming, fishing or industrial work,
that we may render thanks and praise to you;
through Jesus Christ our Lord.

Collects with the New Lectionary

The lessons of the seed 146

Lord Jesus, you taught men the lessons of the seed:
the seed that springs up and grows in ways unknown to men;
the seed that though the smallest becomes a great plant;
the seed that gives its life that new life may be multiplied.

Write these lessons of faith, hope and love on our hearts, that
our lives may yield an abundant harvest in your service, to the
glory of your name. *Basil Naylor*

ASCENSIONTIDE

Acts of worship   **147**

ALMIGHTY and everlasting God, we worship and adore you
because you have exalted your Son our Lord Jesus Christ and
caused him to triumph mightily.

He is the King of glory enthroned at your right hand.

He is our great High Priest who has entered the heavenly
sanctuary to intercede for us.

He is the Lord of the Church to whom all authority has been
given.

To him who sits upon the throne and to the Lamb be praise
and honour, glory and dominion, for ever and ever.

Frank Colquhoun

148

We praise you, O God, because you have exalted your Son
Jesus Christ to your right hand and bestowed on him the name
above all names, that in the name of Jesus every knee should bow.

Wherefore, our Father, accept our homage, our adoration, our
thanksgiving; and grant that we, with those of every tongue, may
confess that Jesus Christ is Lord, to your honour and glory.

Based on Philippians 2. 5–11

149

This day, our God and Father,
we lift up our hearts in joyful praise
and adore your Son our Lord Jesus Christ,

exalted to your right hand in heaven,
    acknowledging him as our triumphant King,
    rejoicing in him as our great High Priest,
    and trusting in him as our only Saviour and Mediator.
To him, with you and the Holy Spirit,
be honour and glory for ever and ever.   *Frank Colquhoun*

Christ the King   150

Grant, Almighty God, that while your Son Jesus Christ is exalted to the throne of heaven, we may not be weighed down by the things of earth, but may set our affection on the things above, where he is seated at your right hand, and lives and reigns with you and the Holy Spirit, one God, now and for ever.

Based on an ancient collect

151

Christ has ascended up on high
    and reigns on the throne of the universe,
    crowned with glory and honour.
For God has highly exalted him and bestowed on him
    the name which is above every name.
He must reign until he has put
    all his enemies under his feet.

Lord Christ, we acknowledge your kingship,
    we worship and adore you.
Accept our homage, come and reign over us,
    and extend your empire over all the world,
that every tongue may confess you Lord,
    to the glory of God the Father.   *Frank Colquhoun*

Christ is the King
to whom all authority has been given
in heaven and on earth.
> We own him as our Lord.
> We yield him our obedience.
> We dedicate our lives to his service.
Come, Lord Christ, and reign in us,
and make us the agents of your kingdom in the world,
to the honour of your name. *Frank Colquhoun*

Our great High Priest 153

Lord God almighty, we magnify your Son Jesus Christ, our great High Priest, who has entered once for all into the heavenly sanctuary and ever lives to plead on our behalf.

Grant that we, sanctified by the offering of his body, may draw near with a true heart in full assurance of faith by the new and living way he has dedicated for us, and present our bodies a living sacrifice.

Through the same our Lord Jesus Christ, who is alive and reigns with you and the Holy Spirit, one God, for ever and ever.

Based on Hebrews 9. 11–12; 10. 10, 19–22

The Man on the throne 154

Lord Jesus, as we rejoice in your return to the glory of heaven, we remember with thankfulness that you took our humanity upon you and now carry it with you into the life eternal, with the scars of your passion still upon you.

Blessed Lord, help us to live in the fullness of the new life you have won for us as children of God, that we may at last share in the glory and worship of heaven.

We ask this for your name's sake. *Norah Field*

The Forerunner 155

We praise you, God our Father, that our ascended Lord has entered heaven as the forerunner of his people and has gone to prepare a place for us, so that where he is, there we may be also.

May the thought that he now reigns at your right hand make heaven a more real and wonderful place to us; and may we be enabled to lay hold more firmly on the hope that is set before us, that we may come at last where he has gone before, through the merits and mediation of his great name. *Frank Colquhoun*

An act of worship **156**

PRAISE to the Holy Spirit who alone enables us to call God our Father and Jesus our Lord.

May we live and walk by the same Spirit,
that we may grow in the likeness of Jesus Christ
and pray with the freedom of the sons of God.

Praise to the Holy Spirit for his fruit of love and joy and peace.

May he put to death in us the works of the flesh,
that his fruit may grow and prosper
and our lives be lived to the glory of God.

Praise to the Holy Spirit for his gifts of power and inspiration.
May he lead the Church to desire the best gifts
and to distinguish the true from the false,
for the sake of the health of the Body.

Praise to the Holy Spirit who is the promise of the Father and the gift of the Son, in whose name we pray, Jesus Christ our Lord.   *Christopher Idle*

Pentecost **157**

Almighty God, your prophet of old spoke of a day when you would do a new thing for your people and pour out your Spirit on all alike.

We praise you that that day dawned for your Church at Penetecost.

We praise you that we are now living in that new age of the Spirit.

May his power cleanse, quicken and inspire our lives and renew the witness of your Church in all the world, to the furtherance of your kingdom and the glory of Christ our Lord.

Frank Colquhoun

Mission and witness   **158**

O God, who on the day of Pentecost enabled your Spirit-filled people so to bear witness to their Lord that men of different races heard the good news in their mother tongue: baptize your Church today with the same Spirit of power, that it may fulfil its mission to preach the gospel to the whole creation and all the peoples of the world may learn of Christ in their own language, to the glory of his name.   *Adapted*

159

O Holy Spirit of God,
   Spirit of truth, of light, of love,
by whom Jesus is made known to us
   and through whom the love of God
   is shed abroad in our hearts:
come upon us in the power of Pentecost,
   to renew in us such gifts and graces
   as will glorify God
and equip us for ministry and witness
   in the Church and in the world;
through Jesus Christ our Lord.   *Llewellyn Cumings*

160

Heavenly Father, by the power of your Holy Spirit
set our hearts on fire with a new love for Christ,
that we may be alive to the opportunities of these times
and bear our witness with urgency and zeal.

Save us from complacency and from fear of new ways:
inspire our minds with the vision of a world won for our Lord;
and stir our wills to pray and work until your will is done.

Adapted

Fellowship 161

We praise you, O God, for the fellowship of the Spirit, who
unites us in the bond of peace as members of the one Body.
Deepen our communion one with another in Christ, and grant
that through your Spirit continually working in us we may
daily increase in the knowledge of your love, and learn to love
our brethren with the love you have shown to us in Jesus Christ
our Lord. *Adapted from Response*

Guidance 162

"When the Spirit of truth comes, he will guide you into all the
truth."

So, Lord Jesus, you have promised, and so we believe.

Open our hearts to receive the Spirit in all his gracious fullness,
and make us sensitive to his guidance, that we may know your
mind and do your will, for your name's sake. *Frank Colquhoun*

Renewal 163

Holy Spirit, Lord God, giver of life, come to us as a refreshing
and strengthening power.

Purge out of our lives all that denies your inspiration.

Keep us alert to your challenges.

Let us be open to your new demands in the world and in the
Church.

Give us humility that we may see the vision, and trusting in
your power may commit ourselves to it, in the name of Christ
our Lord. *Brother John Charles, SSF*

164

Holy Spirit of God, one in the glory of the Father and the Son,
  we worship and adore you.
Spirit of life, source of all power and beauty,
  quicken our lives and renew our strength.
Spirit of truth, illuminating the minds of men,
  reveal to us the hidden things of God.
Spirit of Christ, witnessing to his grace and glory,
  take possession of our lives and make us more like him, our
    Saviour and our Lord.   *Frank Colquhoun*

165

We praise you, O God, because you gave the Holy Spirit to
the first Christians,
  making Jesus real to them,
  teaching them the truth,
  and giving them power to witness boldly.
  Fill us with the same Spirit that we may know their experience
and follow their example, for Jesus' sake.   *Family Worship*

The fruit of the Spirit   **166**

Almighty God, you have taught us in your word
  that the fruit of the Spirit is love.
Give us by your Spirit the realization of that love in our hearts:
  the love that is patient, kind, and envies no one;
  the love that is never boastful, conceited or rude;
  the love that is never selfish, nor quick to take offence;
  the love that does not gloat over other men's sins but delights
    in the truth;
  the love that will last for ever.
Above all else help us, O God our Father,
  to know that Christ is love in person,
  and love is Christ in our hearts.   *Llewellyn Cumings,*
                            Based on 1 Corinthians 13, NEB

O God, empty us of self
   and fill us with your Holy Spirit,
that we may bring forth abundantly
   the fruit of love, joy and peace,
and glorify you day by day
   in lives renewed in the beauty of holiness;
through Jesus Christ our Lord.   *Frank Colquhoun*

TRINITY SUNDAY

Thanksgiving **168**

THANKS be to God our Father, who made us and sustains us through the harvests of the world.

Thanks be to Jesus Christ his Son, who redeemed us and reconciles us to God through the blood of his cross.

Thanks be to God the Holy Spirit, who regenerated us and revives us in the life of the Church.

O God, all-loving, all-holy, all-wise, we worship and adore you. *Maurice A. P. Wood*

Prayer **169**

Father, Son, and Holy Spirit,
   holy and blessed Trinity,
accept and sanctify all that we are,
   all that we have,
   and all that we seek to offer you;
and keep us steadfast in our faith in you,
   our Creator, Redeemer, and Sanctifier,
   one God, for ever and ever. *Adapted*

170

Eternal God, you have revealed yourself to us in your grace as Father, Son, and Holy Spirit, the God of our salvation.

Help us firmly to believe in you, boldly to confess your name, and joyfully to worship you, one holy, glorious and undivided Trinity, for ever and ever. *Frank Colquhoun*

Doxology   **171**

Let us give praise to the Father who by his grace has made us his
    children;
    to the Son who by his death and resurrection has brought us
      new life;
    to the Spirit who dwells in our. hearts and strengthens us for
      service.
    To the holy and blessed Trinity be praise and glory for ever
      and ever.   *Adapted*

172

    Blessing and honour, thanksgiving and praise,
      more than we can utter,
      more than we can conceive,
    be to your glorious name, O God,
      Father, Son, and Holy Spirit,
    by all angels, all men, all creation,
      for ever and ever.   *After Lancelot Andrewes*

173

    To God the Father, Lord of all creation;
    to God the Son, Redeemer of the world;
    to God the Holy Spirit, Sanctifier of the Church:
    to the one holy and undivided Trinity
    be all praise and glory through ages everlasting.

174

    Glory be to God the Father,
      who made us, and all the world.
    Glory be to God the Son,
      who redeemed us, and all mankind.
    Glory be to the Holy Spirit,
      who sanctifies us, and all the people of God.

To the holy, blessed and glorious Trinity,
   three persons and one God,
be all glory and praise, dominion and power,
   now and for evermore.

Based on the Church Catechism

Thanksgiving **175**

ALMIGHTY God, we are taught by your word that for our daily needs we are dependent not only on the work of men's hands but also on your providence and fatherly care.

And so we praise you at this time for your gifts to us in nature by which the earth is enriched and made fruitful, and for the labours of those by whom the harvest is gathered in.

Make us thankful for all that we receive, and teach us that in the whole of life we are workers together with you, the author and giver of all good things; through Jesus Christ our Lord.

Frank Colquhoun

176

God our Father, we thank you for the world and for all your gifts to us: for the sky above, the earth beneath our feet, and the wonderful process which provides food to maintain life.

We thank you for our crops, and for the skills and techniques needed to grow and use them properly.

Help us to use your gifts in the spirit of the giver, through Jesus Christ our Lord.
J. R. Worsdall

177

Father of mercies and Lord of all creation,
we gratefully acknowledge our dependence on your bounty
for all the good things we enjoy.
We thank you at this time for
the fruits of the earth,

the harvest of the sea,
the wealth of the mines,
and for all the beauty of the world in which we live.
Accept our worship and fill our hearts with praise;
through Jesus Christ our Lord.   *Frank Colquhoun*

178

We thank you, Lord, for the beauty and diversity of the world
which you have made to be the home and mother of mankind.

We thank you for making its hospitality to man endless in
interest, loveliness, diversity and utility.

Teach us by your creation to know more of you our Creator,
and rejoicing in you, to be as generous to others as you are to us;
through Jesus Christ our Lord.   *Dick Williams*

Prayer   **179**

Lord of the harvest,
by whose mercy our needs are supplied:
we pray for all who work on the land
and who gather the harvest of the seas;
that they may know the dignity and worth
of their service
and be justly rewarded for their toil;
through Jesus Christ our Lord.   *James M. Todd*

180

At this harvest time, Lord God,
we acknowledge that all good gifts around us
are sent from heaven above.
Help us to receive them gratefully,
to use them wisely
and to share them unselfishly,
as good stewards of your bounty,
for the sake of our Saviour Jesus Christ.
Frank Colquhoun

181

O God, the Creator and Preserver of all mankind, may we never take your gifts for granted but receive them always with thanksgiving.

Enable us to use them wisely and responsibly, and to remember the needs of others, that we may give as freely as we have received; for the sake of Jesus Christ our Lord.   *Adapted*

182

Lord, make us more thankful for what we have received;
make us more content with what we have;
and make us more mindful of other people in need.
We ask it for the sake of him who lived in poverty,
our Saviour Jesus Christ.   *Simon H. Baynes*

See also 141–6

The hungry   **183**

We thank you, Lord and Creator of all things, for the blessings of this life and the abundant variety of your gifts; for the food we eat and the pleasure it gives us.

But we know that millions have less than enough while others eat to excess.

Food is wasted while millions starve.

Nature's resources are misused to bring men profit.

Forgive us, Lord, our selfishness, and open our hearts to the needs of the hungry wherever they may be, for the sake of our Lord Jesus Christ.   *Basil Naylor*

See also 414–19

The use of earth's resources   **184**

We rejoice, O Lord, that you have made the earth so rich in natural resources; and we pray that we may learn to use them responsibly:

not wasting them on what we do not need,
not polluting the soil, the air and the sea,
not wantonly destroying the life of animals and plants;
but taking care to hand on to others an earth fit for the life of
man, to the honour of your name. *Roger Tomes*

185

Almighty God, Creator and Lord of all things, we thank you
for the vast resources of the earth and the sea, and for the hidden
forces of nature now brought within our grasp by scientific
discovery.

Help us to use all your gifts wisely and faithfully for the
benefit of mankind, that all may rejoice in your goodness;
through Jesus Christ our Lord. *Adapted*

186

God our Father, in whom we live and move and have our
being, we thank you for the beauty of creation. May the achieve-
ments of men not disfigure it but enhance it to your greater glory.

We thank you for the wealth of the world's resources. May
they not be squandered or wasted but shared justly among all
people.

Accept our gratitude for all your bounty, and hear our prayer,
for the sake of Jesus Christ our Lord.

Adapted

Reverence for creation 187

Almighty God, we are taught by your word that the whole
universe exists in and through your Son Jesus Christ and is sustained by the energy of your life-giving Spirit.

We pray that this word may lead us into reverence for all your
creation, and guide our understanding and our use of its powers;
through the same Jesus Christ our Lord. *Basil Naylor*

We praise you, Almighty God,
    for creating all things in time and space,
    and for making man in your own image.
Lead us to recognize your hand
    in all that you have created,
and always to praise you
    for your wisdom and love;
through Jesus Christ our Lord,
who with you and the Holy Spirit
reigns supreme over all things,
    now and for ever.   *A Christian's Prayer Book*

189

Lord of the universe, we praise you for your creation:
    for the wonder of space,
    the beauty of the world,
    and the value of earth's resources.
Keep us from spoiling these gifts of yours by our selfishness,
and help us to use them for the good of all men, to the glory of
your name.   *Family Worship*

REMEMBRANCE SUNDAY

The supreme sacrifice **190**

ALMIGHTY God, our heavenly Father, we remember with thanksgiving those who made the supreme sacrifice for us in time of war.

We pray that the offering of their lives may not have been in vain.

By your grace enable us this day to dedicate ourselves anew to the cause of justice, freedom and peace; and give us the wisdom and strength to build a better world, for the honour and glory of your name; through Jesus Christ our Lord.   *Adapted*

191

Almighty God, from whose love in Christ
    we cannot be parted, by death or by life:
hear our prayers and thanksgivings
    for those whom we remember this day.
Fulfil in them the purpose of your love;
    and bring us, with them, to your eternal joy;
through Jesus Christ our Lord.

192

We give thanks this day, O Lord of hosts,
    for all that makes our common life secure;
    for the peace and freedom we enjoy;
and for the opportunity that is ours
    of building a better order of society
    for the generations to come.

We remember with pride and gratitude
   those who fought and died to make this possible;
and we pray that the memory of their sacrifice
   may inspire in us the resolve to seek your kingdom
and to do your will for the world of our day;
   through Jesus Christ our Lord.   *Adapted*

For peace   **193**

On this day of remembrance, O God, as we recall those who died in the service of their country, we pray for the peace of the world.

Guide the leaders of this and every nation and give them understanding of your righteous will; that the tragedy and horror of war may be averted for the coming generation, and men and women everywhere may be able to live in the freedom and fellowship of your kingdom; through Jesus Christ our Lord.

Frank Colquhoun

194

Lord Jesus, you have shown us
how great is the price of freedom
by giving your life to deliver us from evil.
Teach us to give to the uttermost;
   to respect that which others have secured for us;
and to pursue peace in obedience to your will,
until the kingdoms of this world
all give you their full allegiance.   *Roger Pickering*

195

Grant, O Lord, for the sake of those whose lives were lost in war, and for the sake of the generation to come, that the nations of the world may learn your way of peace; and that all men may have a chance to enjoy the life you have given them, free from war, tyranny and oppression.   *Roger Tomes*

196

Grant us grace, O Lord, to learn of your judgments which overtake us when we set brother against brother and nation against nation. Give us wisdom and strength to fashion better instruments for our common life, so that we may dwell in concord under your providence; and may your kingdom come among us, through Jesus Christ our Lord. *Reinhold Niebuhr*

See also 281–91

Act of remembrance

197

Let us remember before God, and commend to his mercy and keeping,
those who have died for their country in war;
those whom we knew, and whose memory we treasure;
and all who have lived and died in the service of mankind.

Here follows the silence

Most gracious God and Father, in whose will is our peace: turn our hearts and the hearts of all men to yourself, that by the power of your Spirit the peace which is founded on righteousness may be established throughout the world; through Jesus Christ our Lord. *Service for Remembrance Sunday*

Those who suffer

198

God our Father, as on this day we look back and remember with gratitude those who died in time of war, so also we look around and remember with compassion those who still suffer as the result of war: the bereaved, the lonely, the disabled, and the mentally ill.

O God of love, comfort their hearts, uphold their faith, and give them peace, for Jesus Christ's sake. *Frank Colquhoun*

199

Let us pray for all who suffer as a result of war:
  for the injured and the disabled,
  for the mentally distressed,
  and for those whose faith in God and in man has been weakened
    or destroyed . . .
  for the homeless and refugees,
  for those who are hungry,
  and for all who have lost their livelihood and security . . .
  for those who mourn their dead,
  those who have lost husband or wife, children or parents,
  and especially for those who have no hope in Christ to sustain
    them in their grief . . .
Almighty God, our heavenly Father, infinite in wisdom, love
and power: have compassion on those for whom we pray; and
help us to use all suffering in the cause of your kingdom, through
him who gave himself for us on the cross, Jesus Christ your Son
our Lord.   *Service for Remembrance Sunday*

200

Father of mercies and God of all comfort, whose Son ministered
to those in need: remember for good all who suffer through war,
by loss of home or faculties, by loss of friends and loved ones, by
loss of security or freedom.

Look upon our world, still torn apart by violence and fighting,
and grant success to those who work for peace; through him who
reconciled men with God, and men with men, the Lord Jesus
Christ.   *Christopher Idle*

See also 310

Commitment 201

Let us pledge ourselves anew to the service of God and our fellow men, that we may help, encourage, and comfort others, and support those working for the relief of the needy and for the peace and welfare of the nations.

> Lord God our Father, we pledge ourselves
> to serve you and all mankind
> in the cause of justice and peace
> and for the relief of want and suffering.
> Guide us by your Spirit;
> give us wisdom, courage, and hope;
> and keep us faithful now and always,
> for the honour of your name.

Service for Remembrance Sunday

St. Andrew (November 30)   **202**

HEAVENLY Father, by whose grace we have been called into
the fellowship and service of your Church: help us to follow
the example of the apostle Andrew who brought his own brother
to Jesus; that we may share the good news of our salvation with
those near to us in our families and our neighbourhood, to the
advancement of your kingdom and the glory of Jesus Christ our
Lord.   *Frank Colquhoun*

                                                                   203

Lord Jesus Christ, who called Andrew from his nets to become
a fisher of men and a messenger of your good news: may we so
find in you our Saviour and our Lord that others through our
testimony may come to put their trust in you and rejoice in your
salvation, to the honour of your name.   *Leo Stephens-Hodge*

St. Thomas (December 21)   **204**

Risen Master, help us, like your apostle Thomas, to be honest
enough to admit our doubts and not to affect a faith we do not
possess; and enable us, like him, so to experience your living
presence and power that our doubts may be dissolved and we may
inherit the blessing promised to those who have not seen you and
yet trust in you, our Lord and our God.   *Frank Colquhoun*

St. Stephen (December 26) 205

Lord Jesus, Son of God, help us by your grace, and through the example of your first martyr Stephen, to be fearless in our witness before a hostile world, and to live and die in your faith; for the glory of your name. *Adapted*

St. John the Evangelist (December 27) 206

Eternal God, who through the witness of the apostle and evangelist Saint John revealed the mystery of the Word made flesh for our salvation: grant that we who rejoice in your love may walk in the light of your truth and be partakers of the life eternal, by faith in your Son Jesus Christ our Lord. *Frank Colquhoun*

The Innocents' Day (December 28) 207

Heavenly Father, you saved your Son from Herod's anger and cruel designs: enable us to understand the plight of all who suffer undeservedly, and through us free the world from cruelty and oppression; for the sake of Jesus Christ our Lord. *Collects with the New Lectionary*

208

Lord Jesus, as we recall at this time the slaughter of the babes of Bethlehem, we think also of the suffering of the young and innocent in our own day; and we confess that our minds are perplexed and our hearts are sad. Yet in face of this great mystery we affirm our faith that God is sovereign and God is love.

Keep us steadfast in this faith; and give your comfort and peace to all who today mourn the loss of children, for your tender mercy's sake. *Frank Colquhoun*

For the Feast of the Circumcision, see 45

The Conversion of St. Paul (January 25) 209

O Lord our God, we thank you for your amazing grace in calling Saul of Tarsus, the enemy and persecutor of the Church, to be Christ's dedicated servant and apostle, and to bear witness to him among the nations.

As today we recall his conversion we pray that we may know the same grace in our own lives, and like him may never be ashamed of the gospel.

We ask it in the name of him who came into the world to save sinners, Jesus Christ our Lord. *Frank Colquhoun*

The Presentation of Christ (February 2) 210

We give you thanks and praise, O God, for the Gospel of the Presentation:

for the wisdom and insight of Simeon and Anna,
for the loving care of Joseph and Mary,
for the simplicity and innocence of the child Jesus.

We pray for the different generations of our own day, that in offering their lives in service to you and to each other they may grow in mutual respect and understanding, and so enrich the life of all, for Jesus Christ's sake. *Basil Naylor*

211

Lord God, you kept faith with Simeon and showed him the infant King: give us grace to put all our trust in your promises, and the patience to wait a lifetime for their fulfilment; through Jesus Christ our Lord. *Susan Williams*

St. Matthias (February 24) 212

Lord Christ, we thank you that in every age
you call faithful men like Matthias to be your witnesses
and to serve you in the apostolic ministry.
Give your grace to those who in our own day
are called to be leaders in your Church,

that they may be loyal to the gospel entrusted to them,
loyal to the people committed to their care,
and above all loyal to yourself, their Master,
to whom be glory for ever and ever.   *Frank Colquhoun*

The Annunciation (March 25)   213

We praise you, our Father, for the marvellous news announced
to Mary;
for the grace of life that prepared her for her call;
for her obedience to your will and her humility in accepting it;
for her loving care and patience in fulfilling it.
Give us such grace and obedience that we may be accounted
worthy to bear the good news to our world; through Jesus
Christ our Lord.   *Basil Naylor*

214

Almighty God, who chose the Virgin Mary to be the mother
of our Lord: we thank you for her trust and love, and for her
ready obedience to your will.
Give us grace to follow the example of her devotion, and to
serve you with pure hearts and minds; through the same Jesus
Christ our Lord.   *Adapted*

St. Mark (April 25)   215

We give thanks, O God, for your servant John Mark: for the
grace by which he triumphed over early failure, and for the
inspiration by which he penned the story of the strong Son of
God.
Teach us through his life and writings the secret of victorious
living, and deepen out faith in your redeeming love and power,
made known to us in Jesus Christ our Lord. *Frank Colquhoun*

Almighty God, we praise you for the good news of Jesus Christ
your Son as told by the evangelist Saint Mark.

Help us in this our day to know that the time is fulfilled, and
that the kingdom of God is upon us; and grant us grace to repent
and believe the gospel; for Jesus' sake.   *Llewellyn Cumings,*
Based on Mark 1. 14–15

St. Philip and St. James (May 1)   217

Almighty God, by whose providence your servants Philip and
James were called to be apostles of our Lord: help us like them so
to follow Jesus as to know him to be the Way; and so to believe
in Jesus as to find in him the Truth; that following and believing
we may possess eternal life through his name.

Llewellyn Cumings

St. Barnabas (June 11)   218

We thank you, Father, for dedicated men and women who like
Barnabas have offered their goods and their gifts to your service,
and their companionship to your servants.

Help us to follow the pattern of their selfless devotion and loyal
friendship, and so to further the cause of your kingdom; for the
glory of our Lord and Saviour Jesus Christ.   *Basil Naylor*

219

Christ our Lord, we remember today with thanksgiving your
servant Barnabas, that generous and warm-hearted man who was
a true Son of Consolation in the apostolic church.

Help us by your grace to follow his faith, the faith that works
through love; and like him, make us generous in our giving, in
our judgments, and in our friendship.

Grant this, O Lord, for the honour of your name.

Frank Colquhoun

The Nativity of St. John Baptist (June 24)   220

By your power, Sovereign Lord, John the Baptist was born into the world as forerunner of the promised Messiah.

Help us to heed his message of repentance and amendment of life, and to follow his example of boldness and self-denial; through Jesus Christ our Lord.

Collects with the New Lectionary

221

Give us, O God, something of the spirit of your servant John the Baptist:

his moral courage,
his contentment with simplicity,
his refusal to be fettered by this world,
his faithfulness in witness to the end.

So may we be heralds of Christ and his kingdom and make ready his way, to the glory of his name.

Adapted from Response

St. Peter (June 29)   222

We praise you, Lord Christ, for your apostle Simon Peter, the man of rock:

for his bold confession of your name;
for his courageous leadership of the apostolic church;
for his abounding zeal in your service;
for his love and loyalty to you, his Lord.

Give us the same rock-like qualities of faith, courage and devotion in your service, and keep us steadfast to the end, for the honour of your great name.   *Frank Colquhoun*

223

Almighty God, who revealed to the apostle Peter the truth about your Son, the promised Messiah, so that he was enabled to make a good confession: give grace to all leaders of your Church today, that they may fulfil their calling with wisdom and courage, and ever build on him who is made the sure foundation, Jesus Christ our Lord. *Frank Colquhoun*

Visitation of the Blessed Virgin Mary (July 2) 224

Lord God, as Mary visited Elizabeth,
to be greeted by her with rejoicing
as the mother of her Lord,
give us joy in all that you have done for us,
and help us to enter into our inheritance
in Jesus Christ our Lord.

Collects with the New Lectionary

St. Mary Magdalen (July 22) 225

Most merciful Father, whose compassion was revealed to Mary of Magdala in transforming power: cast out from our hearts all that is evil and make us new in Christ; and grant us such gratitude for your love that we, like her, may minister to the needs of your people and be witnesses to our risen Lord. In his name we ask it.

Llewellyn Cumings

226

Lord Christ, as you delivered Mary Magdalen
and made her the first witness of the resurrection,
set us free from all that holds us captive,
that we may bear witness to your risen life today.
We ask it in your name, living, reigning Lord.

Collects with the New Lectionary

See also 136

St. James (July 25)   **227**

All praise to you, O God our Father, for James the apostle of Jesus, who drank his Lord's cup of suffering and won the martyr's crown.

Make us, like him, ready to bear the reproach of Christ and to tread the way of the cross, and keep us faithful unto death; through the same Jesus Christ our Lord.   *Frank Colquhoun*

The Transfiguration (August 6)   **228**

Lord Jesus Christ, who appeared in majesty to your disciples on the mountain and spoke of your coming passion: we adore you in the glory of your transfiguration and own you as our crucified Lord; and we pray that we, beholding and reflecting your glory, may be changed into your likeness from one degree of glory to another by the Lord the Spirit, to the praise and honour of your name.   *Frank Colquhoun*

229

God of Moses and Elijah,
Father of Jesus Christ our Lord,
we recall that fearful moment on the mount
when Peter, James and John heard your voice
and saw the touch of glory on your Son.
May we by faith behold his majesty
and give him the obedience and reverence
which are his due;
and to his name be dominion and power
now and for evermore.   *Roger Pickering*

St. Bartholomew (August 24)   **230**

Heavenly Father, as today we commemorate the apostle Bartholomew we bless you for your saints whose names are honoured in the Church but whose deeds are little known.

Accept our praise for all such; and help us so to follow their faith that our lives too may bring you glory, through Jesus Christ our Lord. *Frank Colquhoun*

The Beheading of St. John the Baptist (August 29) 231

Lord God, who sent your servant John the Baptist to bear witness to Christ and to prepare the way of his coming: we praise you for his faithfulness in your service, even unto death; and we pray for grace and courage in this our day to give our lives in the service of truth and righteousness; for the honour of Christ our Lord. *Adapted*

The Nativity of the Blessed Virgin Mary (September 8)

232

Most merciful God, as we commemorate the birth of the mother of our Lord, we thank you for the grace of humility and the spirit of loving obedience shown us in her life.

May we like her always be responsive to your word and submissive to your will, that we may serve you with compassionate hearts and pure minds, to the glory of your name.

Frank Colquhoun

St. Matthew (September 21) 233

O God, who through the record given us by Saint Matthew revealed your Son as the fulfilment of the law and the prophets and as the promised Son of David: grant to us, who are members of the new Israel and acknowledge the kingship of Jesus, the obedience of faith, that we may go and make all nations his disciples, knowing that he is with us always, to the end of time.

Llewellyn Cumings

234

Lord Jesus, you have taught us
that no man can serve both God and mammon:
save us from the love of money,
as you saved your servant Matthew the tax-gatherer
and gave him a new love and a new life;
and lead us through his testimony
to enthrone you as our King.
To your name be glory and dominion for ever and ever.

Frank Colquhoun

St. Michael and All Angels (September 29)   **235**

Almighty God, sovereign of all creation, we praise your name
for men and angels who have joined in the war against the
powers of evil.

Most of all we praise you for the cross of your Son Jesus Christ
which ensures the final victory.

Grant that we who are marked with the sign of that victory
may continue Christ's faithful soldiers and servants to our lives'
end.   *Basil Naylor*

236

Lord of the heavenly hosts, your angels dwell always in your
presence and do all that you command them. Open our eyes to
become aware of this great company; that encouraged by their
example we may serve you faithfully and advance your glory,
till we rejoice in their fellowship; through Jesus Christ our Lord.

Leo Stephens-Hodge

St. Luke (October 18)   **237**

Almighty God, by whose grace your servant Luke, the beloved
physician, was enabled to write in the Gospel of the love and
healing power of your Son: may your Church today show the

same love and power to a world in need by proclaiming the good
news of your salvation, both in word and deed; through Jesus
Christ our Lord.   *Roger Pickering,*
                        Adapted from American Prayer Book

St. Simon and St. Jude (October 28)   **238**

Lord Christ, we thank you that you chose as your apostles
some ordinary and obscure men such as Simon and Jude.

Teach us by their example that it is more important to be
faithful than to be prominent; and help us to serve you at all times
with holy and humble hearts, to the glory of God the Father.
                                            Frank Colquhoun

All Saints (November 1)   **239**

Almighty God, the God not of the dead but of the living: we
praise and bless your holy name for your saints of every time and
place who have served you faithfully in their generation and have
enriched the world by their lives, their witness, and their example.

Help us by your grace to follow them as they followed Christ,
that with them we may be partakers of your everlasting joy;
through the merits of Jesus our Saviour and our Lord.
                                                    Adapted

                                                 240

Lord God Almighty,
   you call men to be your saints
   and unite them in the fellowship of your Church:
   help us in our earthly life
   to follow the example of your saints in heaven,
   and to share with them in the joy of your kingdom;
   through Jesus Christ our Lord.
                        Collects with the New Lectionary

Commemoration of All Souls (November 2) 241

Eternal God, Lord of heaven and earth, we remember with thanksgiving, and commend to your infinite love, those faithful souls who having served you here on earth are now at rest in your presence, especially those most dear to us.

Give us grace so to follow their faith and good examples that we may share their joy, and at last be numbered with your saints in glory everlasting; through the mercy of our Lord and Saviour Jesus Christ.   *Frank Colquhoun*

The Communion of Saints 242

Lord, remember in mercy your Church throughout the world; make all its members to grow in love for you and for one another.

Remember our brothers and sisters who have gone to their rest in the hope of the resurrection to eternal life; and bring us with them into the light of your presence, that in union with all your saints we may give you glory for ever, through your Son Jesus Christ our Lord.

Adapted from a Roman Catholic Requiem

243

Father of all, whose family in heaven and on earth is one: deepen within us our sense of the communion of saints, and give us grace to follow them more nearly in the way of holiness, even as they followed Christ; to whom be glory and dominion for ever and ever.

Saints of England 244

God, whom all the saints adore, assembled in your glorious presence from all places of your dominion; who gathered us far dwellers of the islands into the kingdom of your Son and adorned our country with many shining lamps of holiness: grant us worthily to celebrate the saints of England and to follow their good examples, till we all fulfil our destiny in Christ; to whom with you and the Holy Spirit be all honour and glory, now and for ever.

EMBER DAYS

The increase of the ministry 245

ALMIGHTY God, we praise you for those whom you have
called to the ministry of your Church from age to age.
Make known your will to those whom you would use today.
Give them understanding of the task that awaits them;
strengthen them as they prepare to fulfil their calling;
and ever keep them humble and faithful in your service; for
the glory of our Lord and Saviour Jesus Christ. *Adapted*

246

Raise up, O God, for the work of the ministry,
men of spiritual maturity and strong faith;
men of wide vision and sound judgment;
and above all men with a deep love for their Lord
and for their fellows;
that your Church may be served in days to come
by those whose lives are wholly dedicated
to the furtherance of your kingdom;
through Jesus Christ our Lord. *Frank Colquhoun*

247

O God, you have told us to pray
for more labourers in your harvest-field.
We ask you then to call many of your sons
to the work of the ministry,
and to enable them by your grace
to hear and act upon your call.

Make them at all times sensitive to your guidance,
  willing to learn and eager to serve.
We ask this in the name of him who came
  not to be ministered to but to minister,
  Jesus Christ your Son our Lord.   *ACCM*

248

O Christ our High Priest
  and Shepherd of souls,
give to your Church Christlike pastors
  baptized with your Spirit,
  inspired by your truth,
  and filled with your love,
for your own name's sake.   *Ember Prayer*

Those in training   **249**

Lord of the harvest, we pray for those training to become
pastors and teachers in your Church.
  Give them a deepening assurance of your call,
  an increasing experience of your life-giving Spirit,
  a strong conviction of revealed truth
  and a holy boldness to make it known;
  that they may equip your people for work in your service and
build up the body of Christ in faith and knowledge, to the glory
of your great name.   *Michael Botting*

Those newly ordained   **250**

Thank you, Lord, for continuing to call men to the ordained
ministry.
  For those who are being ordained at this time we ask for
courage and patience, joy, and above all for compassion.
  May they grow in love for you and their fellow men, and so
make your infinite love a living reality in the world of our day.

As you gave all you had for us, so help them to give themselves
wholly in love and prayer and service.   *ACCM*

251

Grant, Lord, to those now called to the sacred ministry
confidence in the gospel and the Word of life,
compassion for the lost and needy,
courage, endurance, and unfailing love.
For Jesus Christ's sake.   *Timothy Dudley-Smith*

Ministers of Christ   **252**

Lord Christ, everlasting Son of the Father,
   who for our sake humbled yourself
   and took the form of a servant:
give to all ministers of the gospel
   the spirit of lowly service
   and self-denying love;
and make them to know that in ministering to others
   they are serving you, their only Master,
   for the glory of your name.   *Frank Colquhoun*

253

Heavenly Father, we pray that all who serve you in the
ministry of your Church may fulfil their calling in dependence on
your grace and in harmony with your will; that by the power of
the Holy Spirit they may accomplish all that you would have
them to do, and work not for results or for their own advancement, but wholly for the honour and glory of your name;
through Jesus Christ our Lord.   *Adapted*

254

Strengthen by your Spirit, O Lord God,
   all ministers of your Church,

that they may be leaders of men
    in honesty of thought,
    simplicity of life,
    and sincerity of faith,
and so become faithful shepherds of Christ's flock,
    to the glory of his name.

255

Help your servants, Lord,
    to be men of God,
    men of reconciliation,
    men of truth,
    men of prayer;
    and keep them humble in your service,
      for your mercy's sake.

256

O God, you have chosen men
    to serve you in the ministry of your Church
and have given them a perfect example
    in the person of your Son Jesus Christ.
We ask your blessing
    on all bishops, priests and deacons
      (*especially* . . .).
Let them never forget the privilege of their calling,
    nor shirk its responsibilities.
Keep them in your love, that they may be
    good shepherds of your people
and true servants of him
    who is our great High Priest,
    Jesus Christ our Lord.   *ACCM*

See also 543–6

The apostolic ministry 257

    We thank you, God our Father,
    that from the days of the apostles
    you have chosen and prepared men
    to exercise leadership and oversight in the Church,
    to guard its faith and guide its life.
    We pray for those who in our own day
    are called to the apostolic ministry,
    that they may be holy and humble men of heart,
    strong and courageous,
    sensitive to the Church's needs;
    and may they so exercise their responsibilities
    that your people may be built up in faith and knowledge
    and equipped for work in your service;
    through Jesus Christ our Lord.   *Frank Colquhoun*

The prophetic ministry 258

    Lord, send us prophets in the Church today,
    as in the days of old,
    to make known your living truth
    in the power of the Holy Spirit.
    Give them a clear vision of your purpose
    for the life of the world;
    enable them to speak the Word with all boldness;
    and through their voice recall your people
    to simpler discipleship,
    to holier living,
    and to more dedicated service,
    for the glory of our Lord Jesus Christ.
                        Frank Colquhoun

259

O Lord our God, grant that the Spirit of wisdom, power and love may rest upon all those who have been called to be ministers of the Word in your Church; that the truth you give them to declare may search the conscience, convince the mind, and win the heart of those who hear it, to the glory of your name; through Jesus Christ our Lord.   *Scripture Union Prayers*

The evangelistic ministry   260

Lord Christ, your last word to your disciples
before you left this earth
was that they should go and preach the gospel
in all the world and to every nation.
We praise you for all who since then
have obeyed your command,
and for those who brought the gospel
to our own shores.
Help us to be your witnesses today;
show us how to make the good news meaningful
to our own generation and in our own community;
and may its power be seen more clearly in our lives,
for the honour and praise of your name.

Frank Colquhoun

The pastoral ministry   261

Pour out your Holy Spirit, O Lord,
on all whom you have called to serve your Church
as pastors and teachers.
Give them wise and understanding hearts;
fill them with a true love for your people;
make them holy and keep them humble;

that they may be faithful shepherds
and feed the flock committed to their care,
ever seeking your glory
and the increase of your kingdom;
through Jesus Christ our Lord.   *Frank Colquhoun*

A ministers' conference   **262**

O Lord our heavenly Father, by whose grace we have been
called to be ambassadors for Christ and ministers of his gospel:
direct us now as we take counsel together in the service of your
Church.

Bring all our plans and purposes into line with your perfect will.

Show us how to adapt ourselves and our ministry to the chang-
ing pattern of life today.

Give us fresh encouragement and new vision; and so strengthen
us by your Holy Spirit that we may not falter or fail in the tasks
you are calling us to do.

So may your name be glorified in all things, through Jesus
Christ our Lord.   *Adapted*

II
PRAYERS OF INTERCESSION

OPENING AND CLOSING PRAYERS

The presence of God   **263**

LORD, we come to you in the assurance that you are present
with us now.
  We do not have to seek your presence.
  We are daily living in your presence.
  Make us aware of it.
  Make it real to us.
  And help us in these moments of prayer to know that we are
speaking to one who is near and not far off, whose love is all
around us and who knows our every need.
  We ask it through our Saviour Jesus Christ.

Frank Colquhoun

                                                              264

  Almighty God and Father, help us to be still in your presence,
that we may know ourselves to be your people, and you to be
our God; through Jesus Christ our Lord.   *James M. Todd*

Teach us to pray   **265**

Lord, teach us to pray.
  Help us to come with boldness to the throne of grace.
  Make us conscious of your presence in our midst.
  Give us the freedom of the Holy Spirit.
  Enlarge our vision and increase our faith.
  And may our words and our thoughts be now acceptable in
your sight, O Lord, our rock and our redeemer.

Frank Colquhoun

Before intercession **266**

We lift up our hearts and minds in prayer
in the faith of God the Father, who loves us and knows our
every need;
in the name of God the Son, our Advocate with the Father,
who ever lives to intercede for us;
in the power of God the Holy Spirit, who comes to the aid of
our weakness and pleads within our hearts.
Hear us in your mercy, O God, Father, Son, and Holy Spirit,
for the honour and glory of your name.

Frank Colquhoun

267

Almighty God, perfect in holiness and power, we are not
worthy to speak to you because of our disloyalty and dis-
obedience; yet your Word declares that you graciously accept us
in Jesus Christ your Son our Saviour.

Strengthen our faith in that word, that we may pray to you
with confidence as we come to you now in his name.

Basil Naylor

268

Eternal God and Father, Lord of our lives,
forgive all that hinders our communion with you
and with one another;
that our worship may be in the fellowship of the Spirit
and in the name of your Son,
Jesus Christ our Lord. *Basil Naylor*

269

Lord, save us from being self-centred in our prayers
and teach us to remember to pray for others.
And may we be so bound up in love
with those for whom we pray

that we may feel their needs as acutely as our own,
    and intercede for them with sensitiveness,
    with understanding and with imagination.
This we ask in Christ's name.

Based on words of John Calvin

270

Lord Christ, as members of your Body
    you have made us also members one of another:
help us now, by the aid of the Holy Spirit,
    to forget ourselves
    and to feel the burden of others' needs.
Then, O Lord, through our prayers
    minister your grace and power to them
as you see is most for their good,
    and in accordance with your will,
for the glory of your name.   *Frank Colquhoun*

After prayer   **271**

The things, good Lord, that your servants have prayed for,
give us grace also to work for; and in the purpose of your love
both answer our prayers and prosper our endeavours; for Jesus
Christ our Saviour's sake.   *Frank Colquhoun*

272

Heavenly Father, graciously receive these our prayers, whether
spoken with our lips or echoed in our hearts; and answer them as
may be best for us and those for whom we have prayed, for the
sake of Jesus Christ our Lord.   *Frank Colquhoun*

273

O God of love, say Amen to our prayers, if it be your gracious
will; but if in anything we have asked or done amiss, pardon our
infirmities and answer our necessities, for Jesus and his mercies'
sake.   *After Thomas Wilson*

274

Almighty God, by whose grace we have made our requests known to you in unity of spirit, and whose promise is that our prayers shall be answered when asked in your Son's name: graciously fulfil the desires of our hearts and the petitions of our lips, as may be most for our good; and grant us in this world knowledge of your truth, and in the world to come life everlasting.   *A modern version of the prayer of Saint Chrysostom*

Closing prayers   **275**

> Lord God, whose we are and whom we serve,
>   help us to glorify you
>   in all the thoughts of our hearts,
>   in all the words of our lips,
>   and in all the works of our hands,
>   as becomes those who are your servants,
>   through Jesus Christ our Lord.

276

> Grant us, heavenly Father,
>   reverence, as we recall your glory,
>   understanding, as we recall your compassion,
>   and gratitude, as we recall your goodness;
> so that we may go forth from this service
>   with our knowledge deepened,
>   with love rekindled,
>   and with strength to live better lives;
> through Jesus Christ our Lord.

277

> Father, give to us, and to all your people,
>   in times of anxiety, serenity;
>   in times of hardship, courage;

in times of uncertainty, patience;
  and at all times a quiet trust in your wisdom and love,
through Jesus Christ our Lord.   *Frank Colquhoun*

278

God Almighty bless us with his Holy Spirit;
  guard us in our going out and coming in;
  keep us steadfast in his faith,
  free from sin and safe from danger;
  through Jesus Christ our Lord.

279

May our Lord Jesus Christ
  be near us to defend us,
  within us to refresh us,
  around us to preserve us,
  before us to guide us,
  above us to bless us;
  who lives and reigns with the Father and the Holy Spirit, God
for evermore.

Doxology   **280**

To you, our heavenly Father,
  to you, our Saviour Jesus Christ,
  to you, the Lord the Spirit,
    let all the world give thanks,
    and to your name be glory for evermore.

THE NATIONS OF THE WORLD

Peace of the world 281

G OD of the nations, whose kingdom rules over all,
have mercy on our broken and divided world.
Shed abroad your peace in the hearts of men
and banish from them the spirit that makes for war;
that all races and peoples may learn to live
as members of one family
and in obedience to your laws;
through Jesus Christ our Lord. *Frank Colquhoun*

282

O God, whose purpose of love embraces the whole world, send peace upon earth, that the nations no longer may prepare for war, and that they may try not to destroy but to understand each other.
Take away all bitterness and hatred, and grant that men of all colours and races may learn to live in fellowship together; through Jesus Christ our Lord. *William Barclay★*

283

God of righteousness, God of peace,
forgive the selfishness, greed and arrogance
that cause us to be at enmity one with another.
Help us and all men to live together
in charity and goodwill;
and teach the nations of the world
the things that belong to their peace;
through Jesus Christ our Lord. *Frank Colquhoun*

284

Father of all, we are your family,
and you call us to live together as brothers.
Help us to overcome the barriers that divide us
as men and nations one from another.
Bless every effort being made
to bring peace and understanding to the world,
so that we may learn your ways
and serve your will,
in the name of Jesus Christ our Lord.

Roger Pickering

285

God our Father, you meant men to live as brothers.

Take from us all hatred, suspicion, fear and distrust, and draw us into closer fellowship one with another.

Show us how to use the freedom you have given us for the establishment of your kingdom; and make us instruments of your peace in our homes, our neighbourhood, our country and the world; through Jesus Christ our Lord.   *Adapted*

286

Lord God, you want the well-being of men
and not their destruction.
Take all violence from our midst
and extinguish hatred in our hearts.
Curb the passion in us
that makes us seek each other's lives.
Give peace on earth,
to us and all mankind.
We ask this through Jesus Christ our Lord.

287

Lord, give to the nations wisdom to understand the things that belong to their peace and the will to reject the things that make for war. And we pray that, realizing our common humanity, we may live together as a family and make the world a home, bearing one another's burdens, ministering to one another's needs, and obeying your laws in righteousness, as children of one God and Father in Jesus Christ our Lord.   *George Appleton**

288

O God of love, in whose will is our peace, so set your peace in the hearts of men that the nations of the world may learn to live as members of one family and children of one God and Father, to the glory of your name; through Jesus Christ our Lord.

Adapted

289

Heavenly Father, may your Holy Spirit lead the rich nations to support the poor, and the strong nations to protect the weak, so that every nation may develop in its own way and work together with other nations in true partnership for the promotion of peace and the good of all mankind; through Jesus Christ our Lord.

*Diocese of Melanesia**

290

Almighty God, King and Judge of all mankind, look in pity upon the nations oppressed by strife, bitterness and fear.

We acknowledge our share in the sins which have brought us so often to the brink of destruction.

May your goodness lead us to repentance, that we may yet be spared.

Restrain the pride, the passions and the follies of men, and grant us your grace, mercy and peace; through Jesus Christ our Saviour.

John R. W. Stott

Temper, O Lord, the pride of the nations.

Depose all cruel and ruthless rulers, and free the oppressed peoples of the world.

Remove all fantasies of racial superiority, and clinging to dreams of departed glory.

Make us messengers of peace in a world of strife, and messengers of strife in a world of false peace.

Grant that we and all the nations of the world may follow the things that make for true peace based on justice and love.

For Jesus Christ's sake. *John Kingsnorth*

Racial harmony 292

God and Father of all, who made of one blood all nations of men to dwell on the face of the earth: deepen our understanding of peoples of other races, languages and customs than our own.

Teach us to view them in the light of your own all-embracing love and creative purpose; and give us a vision of the true brotherhood of mankind, united under one Father.

We ask this in the name of him who died that all men might be one, even Jesus Christ our Lord. *Adapted*

293

God of peace, look in mercy upon the sons of men and increase the spirit of sympathy and understanding between those of different race or colour. Strengthen the love of justice and liberty among all people, and bring the whole earth to acknowledge your sovereignty of love and truth; through Jesus Christ our Lord. *New Every Morning*

294

God and Father of mankind, who in your love made all the nations of the world to be one family: help those of different races to love and understand one another better. Take away hatred, jealousy and prejudice, so that all may work together for the coming of your kingdom of righteousness and peace; through Jesus Christ our Lord.

Based on a prayer by Evelyn Underhill

295

Lord God, Creator and Father of us all, you have made of one blood all races and nations of men:

increase among us the spirit of sympathy and understanding, of tolerance and goodwill;

that the prejudices, arrogance and pride which cause division between those of different race or colour may be done away, and all peoples may live together in unity and peace; through Jesus Christ our Lord. *James M. Todd*

Rulers and statesmen **296**

Lord God, we pray that your Holy Spirit may rest on all who bear responsibility for government among the nations. Give them wisdom, courage and strength, that they may make and maintain a true and lasting peace, and that the peoples of the world may dwell together without enmity and without fear, to the glory of your name. *New Every Morning*

297

O God, give to the rulers of this land,
    and to all the leaders of the nations,
the vision to look beyond racial ambitions
    and national boundaries;
that in obedience to your laws,
    and with concern for the needs of others,

they may bring their gifts and treasures
   into the common service of your kingdom,
and so promote the unity of all mankind,
      to the glory of your name.   *Harold E. Evans**

298

Almighty God, we pray for those who occupy high office in the nations of the world. Help them to govern wisely and well; to seek the welfare of all their people; and to make their contribution to the stability, well-being and peace of the world; through Jesus Christ our Lord.   *Roger Tomes*

299

Sovereign Lord of men and nations, we pray for rulers and statesmen who are called to leadership among their fellow countrymen.
   Give them vision to see far into the issues of their time,
   courage to uphold what they believe to be right,
   and integrity in their words and motives;
   and may their service to their people promote the welfare and peace of mankind; through Jesus Christ our Lord.
                                             Basil Naylor

300

Lord, in whose hands are the destinies of the nations: we pray for all who exercise the power of government over the peoples. Make them defenders of liberty and champions of justice; and so rule in their hearts that they may also be lovers and makers of peace; through him who is the Prince of Peace, our Saviour Jesus Christ.   *Worship Now*

301

We pray, O God, for the leaders of the nations; that building
on the foundations of justice, truth and freedom, they may unite
men everywhere in the bonds of peace, for the glory of your
name.   *New Every Morning*

United Nations' Organization   302

Lord God, whose will it is that men should live in peace and
unity: bless the United Nations' Organization and all those who
work within it and in support of it; that succeeding generations
of humanity may be saved from the scourge of war, and the
nations of the world may learn to combine their efforts for the
common good of all mankind; through Jesus Christ our Lord.

303

God and Father of all, who created mankind in your own
image but with many differences of character and culture: we
pray for those who represent their countries in the United
Nations' Organization; that through their counsels each nation
may reach its own maturity, and the whole world may realize
a unity rich enough to express all the manifold variety of your
creation; through Jesus Christ our Lord.   *Basil Naylor*

304

God and Father of mankind, we ask your blessing on the
United Nations' Organization; that through it righteousness may
be established in international relationships, fear and suspicion
may be removed, and a lasting peace ensured; through him who
has shown to man the ways of justice, mercy and peace, your Son
our Saviour Jesus Christ.

305

God and Father of all, grant your blessing to the United
Nations' Organization; that by wise leadership, and the support
of men of every nation, it may establish goodwill and understanding among all people, delivering them from the tyranny of
war into the freedom of peace; through Jesus Christ our Lord.

God's world 306

Lord, you have taught us that the world is yours and those who
dwell on it. Hear us therefore as we pray for the life of the world:
    that every nation may seek the way that leads to peace;
    that human rights and freedom may everywhere be respected;
    and that the earth's resources may be ungrudgingly shared
        among all men.
We ask this through Jesus Christ our Lord.
A Christian's Prayer Book

God's kingdom 307

Almighty God, we long for the time when your kingdom shall
come on earth: when men and nations shall acknowledge your
sovereignty, seek your glory, and serve your good and righteous
will.

Help us not only to pray but also to work for that new day;
and enable us by your grace to promote the cause of justice and
peace, truth and freedom, both in our own society and in the life
of the world; for the honour of Christ, our Saviour and our
Lord. *Frank Colquhoun*

In time of disaster 308

God of goodness and love, in whom we can trust in every hour
of need: have mercy on all who are faced with fear and distress
[through earthquake, tempest, pestilence, flood . . .].

We ask that help may be given to them speedily, and that this emergency may be turned into an opportunity to strengthen the bonds of love and service which bind men and nations together; through Jesus Christ our Lord.

*Christian Aid**

309

Lord of compassion and power, be with those who have survived this disaster, and minister to their needs of body, mind and spirit.

Heal and help those who are injured;

give peace to the dying;

comfort and support the bereaved;

and to all who are working to bring relief and restore order, give strength and resilience to do their work well; for the sake of Jesus Christ our Lord. *Dick Williams*

War victims 310

O God our Father, we bring to you in our prayers those who suffer in body or mind as a result of war, or because of the fear and suspicions that separate nation from nation, race from race, and man from man.

We pray also for all refugees, and for those who have lost wife or husband, children or parents, livelihood, security, or home.

Have mercy upon them, O God, and prosper all who seek to help them in their need, for the sake of Jesus Christ our Lord.

Adapted

In time of crisis 311

God of all wisdom and might, we pray for those involved in the present crisis in . . ., especially those who bear the responsibility and exercise the authority of leadership.

May the Holy Spirit so direct their counsels and actions that justice and mercy may prevail, evil be averted and harmony restored, to the honour of your great name; through Jesus Christ our Lord. *Frank Colquhoun*

Nuclear energy

God of all wisdom and power, ever revealing yourself to those who seek you: grant that men may not only discover the secrets of your universe but may use them according to your will, not for destruction and war, but for the welfare of all your people. We ask this in the name of Jesus Christ our Lord.

George Appleton

Those in authority 313

Lord God of our fathers, whose faithfulness knows no end, we pray for our Queen and for all those under her who guide and govern the affairs of our nation.

Fill them with the fear of your holy name that they may be set free from the fear of man.

Help them in every situation to know and do the thing that is right.

And overrule all their deliberations for the good of our people, and for your glory; through Jesus Christ our Lord.

Frank Colquhoun

314

We pray, O God, for your servant Elizabeth our Queen, for the ministers of the Crown and all members of Parliament. Guide those who rule over us and help them to govern in your faith and fear; and enable them so to order our national life that selfishness and injustice may be defeated, and all may strive together for the common good; to the praise and honour of your name.

*Scripture Union Prayers**

315

God Almighty, Lord of men and nations,
    look with your mercy on our country.
Give grace and wisdom to Elizabeth our Queen,
    her ministers of state
      and all in authority under her;
and so direct their counsels

and guide their decisions
that we may be led into the ways
of justice, freedom and peace,
to the honour of your great name;
through Jesus Christ our Lord.   *Adapted*

316

God and Father of us all, graciously bless this our nation, and
send out your light and your truth to lead us in the paths of justice
and peace.

Give wisdom to those who exercise authority in the government of our land;
remove all causes of contention and strife among us;
unite us in the service of your kingdom;
and make us a God-fearing people, regarding your laws and
living together in brotherly love and concord;
through Jesus Christ our Lord.   *Adapted*

317

God bless our land;
God guide our rulers;
God resolve our differences;
God revive our churches;
God forgive our selfishness;
God protect our homes;
God strengthen our faith;
through Jesus Christ our Lord.
Maurice A. P. Wood

318

We pray, Lord God, for this our nation:
for Elizabeth our Queen,
the Prime Minister,
the members of the Cabinet,
the representatives of the people,

121

the judges and magistrates,
    and all those in authority;
and we pray that you will so rule their hearts
that they may wisely and justly fulfil their trust,
for our good and for your greater glory;
    through Jesus Christ our Lord. *Adapted*

The British Commonwealth 319

We give thanks, O Lord our God, for the peoples of many races, languages and cultures who are bound together with us in the British Commonwealth of nations under our most gracious Queen.

Deepen our understanding of one another's needs; strengthen among us the spirit of mutual responsibility and service as members of one family; and unite us all in the cause of justice, in the love of freedom, and in the quest for peace and order; through Jesus Christ our Lord. *Frank Colquhoun*

The Queen 320

O Lord our governor, we pray for your servant Elizabeth, set over us in your providence to be our Queen.

Give her grace and wisdom to fulfil the varied duties of her calling;
    enrich her in the life of her family and home;
and may she always be a source of strength and inspiration to her people, and promote your honour and glory; through Jesus Christ our Lord. *Frank Colquhoun*

The Royal family 321

Almighty God, Father of all mercies and giver of all grace, we ask your blessing on the members of the Royal family as they fulfil their service among us; that both by their word and example our nation and commonwealth may be strengthened in the love of righteousness and freedom, and preserved in unity and peace; through Jesus Christ our Lord. *Adapted*

Parliament 322

Eternal Lord God, to whom belong all power and dominion: we seek the guidance of your Spirit for all on whom the responsibility of government is laid, and especially for those who serve in the High Court of Parliament; that they may have wisdom to order the affairs of our nation in accordance with your will and for the glory of your name. *ames M. Todd*

323

Almighty God, direct the hearts and minds of those who bear in their hands the government of this people.

Make them to uphold honour and justice,

to restrain evil and oppression,

and to seek the true prosperity of our nation and the welfare of mankind;

through Jesus Christ our Lord. *Timothy Dudley-Smith*

324

Hear us, O Lord our God, as we pray for those who represent us in the Parliament of our nation and for those who serve in places of influence and authority.

Amid all the pressures brought upon them may they follow your guidance and seek to do the thing that is right; that through them your will may be done for this nation, to the honour of your name; through Jesus Christ our Lord.

Frank Colquhoun

Judges and Magistrates 325

Almighty God, Judge eternal and most merciful Saviour, give to the judges and magistrates of our land the humility, insight and compassion needful to those who pass judgment on their fellow men, and the courage always to uphold the cause of truth and justice; through Jesus Christ our Lord. *Basil Naylor*

Those who influence others 326

We pray, O God, for those who as writers, speakers and entertainers influence the thought of our people through the press, radio and television.

Help them to exercise their gifts with responsibility and understanding, that they may enrich the common life of the nation and strengthen the forces of truth and goodness; through Jesus Christ our Lord. *Frank Colquhoun*

Foreign policy 327

God and Father of all, you have taught us to care for one another and to live in peace: grant that our policies towards other nations may be dictated not by self-interest but by concern for the common good, and that we may seek to further the cause of justice and freedom in the world; through Jesus Christ our Lord. *James M. Todd*

The forces of the Crown 328

O God our Father, we pray for all who serve our country as sailors, soldiers and airmen. Grant that meeting danger with courage, and all occasions with discipline and loyalty, they may truly serve the cause of justice and peace, for the honour of your name. *New Every Morning*

Before an election 329

Direct the minds and wills, O God, of the people of this country at the present time; that men and women of integrity and ability, strong, upright and compassionate, may be chosen to represent us in the High Court of Parliament; and give to us, now and always, the blessing of a wise and just government, to lead our nation in the ways of freedom and peace; through Jesus our Lord. *Frank Colquhoun*

330

Lord, you created us free to choose and made us accountable
to you and to each other: give to those of us who have the right
to elect representatives to serve in the government of our country
[or city, borough] an urgent sense of our responsibility, a clear
and unbiased judgment, and a generous concern for the good of
all men; through Jesus Christ our Lord.   *Basil Naylor*

Immigrants   **331**

God of the nations, to whose love all men are of equal dignity
and worth: we pray for immigrants and exiles who have made
their home in this land.

May their coming among us be a benefit both to them and to
our nation; and help us to work together with them to build here
an order of society founded on brotherhood and justice.

We ask it in the name of Christ our Lord.   *Adapted*

In time of national anxiety   **332**

O God, our refuge and strength in every hour of need, raise up
among us at this time faithful and fearless men who know that in
loyalty to your word and will alone can a nation find true peace
and security.

To such and to all in authority give a right judgment and the
courage to follow your way, whatever the cost; for the good of
this people, and for the honour of your name.

Adapted

333

God and Father of us all,
    who through the self-sacrifice of your Son
reconciled the world to yourself,
    and charged us with the ministry of your peace:
by the healing influence of your Spirit
    inspire and direct those who are called to bring
    reconciliation to areas of strife and discord;

that through their ministry
　　men may learn to give and forgive,
　　to listen and to love,
after the example of your Son,
　　Jesus Christ our Lord.　　　　　　　*Basil Naylor*

334

Grant, O Lord, that the men and women of our nation may devote themselves to the common cause, not seeking gain for themselves, but giving much and taking little; that in this time of testing we may all know the joy of service and the discipline of self-denial; for the sake of him who gave himself for us, our Saviour Jesus Christ.　　　　　　　*Adapted*

In time of national disaster　　　　　　　**335**

God, our refuge and strength, a very present help in trouble, we bring to you in our prayers those who are now suffering as a result of . . .

Support and comfort them in their distress; and give them the courage to endure and the faith to overcome; through the love and power of Jesus Christ our Lord.　　　　　*Frank Colquhoun*

In time of national mourning　　　　　　　**336**

Look graciously upon us, O Lord our God, in this time of our nation's sorrow and loss.

Give us comfort, keep us steadfast, uphold our faith; and enable us to find in you our refuge and strength, now and always.　　　　　　　*Frank Colquhoun*

SOCIETY AND INDUSTRY

Social justice

H OLY Spirit, fountain of light and truth, nelp us to understand the causes of our social tensions and unrest.
Open our eyes to economic wrongs and racial bias;
deepen our concern for the poor, the old, and the handicapped;
and stir in us all a burning sense of responsibility one for
another,
as servants of Jesus Christ our Lord. *Basil Naylor*

338

Heavenly Father, whose Son was manifested that he might
destroy the works of the devil:
strengthen the hands of all who are contending against the
forces of evil in the world of our day and are striving to do your
will;
that we and all our fellow men may enjoy the blessings of a
just order of society and live together in freedom and peace;
through Jesus Christ our Lord. *Frank Colquhoun*

339

O God, whose Son Jesus Christ
cared for the welfare of everyone
and went about doing good:
grant us the imagination and perseverance
to create in this country and throughout the world
a just and loving society
for the family of man;

and make us agents of your compassion to the suffering,
    the persecuted and oppressed,
through the Spirit of your Son,
    who shared the sufferings of men,
        our pattern and redeemer, Jesus Christ.

Norwich Cathedral

340

Help us, O God, to understand what your will is in the confusion and unrest of our times.

Give us insight to distinguish between the signs of your Spirit demanding change and renewal, and the signs of human greed and lust for power; that we may be your fellow workers in creating an order of society which acknowledges your sovereign power and might; through Jesus Christ our Lord.

Basil Naylor

341

We bring to you, O God, a world where much is amiss because your will is not done:
    a world where men are at war with one another,
    where the hungry are not fed,
    where people suffer because of their colour,
    where the love of many has grown cold.
We confess our own share in all this and ask for your forgiveness.

Give us understanding of your will, fill us with your fear, and lead us in the right way, for your name's sake. *Roger Tomes*

342

O Lord, we pray that you will hasten the time when no man shall live in contentment while he knows that others have need.

Inspire in us and in men of all nations the desire for social justice, that the hungry may be fed, the homeless welcomed, the sick healed, and a just and peaceful order established in the world, according to your gracious will, made known in Jesus Christ our Lord.   *George Appleton*

343

Father, forgive us that we so often offend:
   by vandalism against your creation;
   by cruelty against your children, our fellow beings;
   by rebellion against your rule of love.
Help us instead to reverence all your works;
to recognize the dignity and worth of every human being;
and to work without ceasing for justice and mercy among all
    peoples.
We ask it in the name of Christ our Lord.

Law and order   344

Lord God, King of righteousness and peace, we pray for those who are responsible for maintaining law and order in our society. Help them to be diligent in their duties and impartial in their judgment, so that through their work the forces of wickedness may be defeated, the cause of truth and justice promoted, and the life of the community safeguarded; through Jesus Christ our Lord.   *Adapted*

The police   345

Lord God, we remember before you the men and women serving in all ranks of the police forces of our land. Give them courage and resolution in times of crisis and danger, and skill, perseverance and good humour in all that they have to do.

May those who exercise command remember always that they are your servants; may those whom they direct act always as men and women under authority; and help us all by thought

and deed constantly to encourage them in the faithful discharge
of their calling; through Jesus Christ our Lord.

D. R. Woodman,
West Yorkshire Police

The social services 346

We thank you, O God, for all who work in the social services:
for policemen and probation officers;
for youth leaders and school teachers;
for welfare officers and psychiatric social workers;
for doctors and nurses and many others.
We pray that you will give to all such people sympathy and
understanding, love and firmness, and the deeper knowledge that
Jesus Christ is the only one who can make men truly whole.
We ask this for his sake, our Saviour and our Lord.

Peter Markby

Industry 347

Almighty and everlasting God, we pray for those engaged in
the industrial life of our nation.
Remove bitterness, distrust and prejudice between employers
and employees.
Give to all a spirit of tolerance, and an earnest desire to seek
for justice and equity, that they may work together for the
common good; through Jesus Christ our Lord.

W. A. Hampton*

348

O God our Father, whose Son Jesus Christ
worked in the carpenter's shop at Nazareth,
we pray for all engaged in industry,
and especially for those in local industry.

Grant increase of understanding and co-operation
    between management and labour,
that together they may seek what is just and wise
    and work in harmony for the benefit of mankind;
through Jesus Christ our Lord.

Scripture Union Prayers★

Industrial disputes 349

O God our Father, teach your servants to resolve their differences fairly and without bitterness; that our industry and commerce may prosper in peace, and the ordered life of our country be maintained; through Jesus Christ our Lord.

Ronald Entwistle

Those whose work is dangerous 350

Most merciful Father, we commend to your care and protection those whose work is dangerous, and especially those who risk their lives for the lives of others.

We thank you for their courage and their devotion to duty; and we pray that in every hour of need they may know that you are with them and may fear no evil.

We ask it in the name of Jesus Christ our Lord.

Frank Colquhoun

(*The above prayer is suitable for firemen, lifeboat crews, members of the armed forces, and others.*)

Farmers 351

Almighty Father, as we acknowledge our dependence on your bounty for our daily bread, so we also seek your blessing on those engaged in agriculture, who plough and sow and reap; and we pray that you will so prosper their work that the earth may yield its full harvest and the needs of all men may be supplied; through Jesus Christ our Lord.   *Frank Colquhoun*

The good earth 352

We thank you, Lord of all creation, for the wonder of the world in which we live: for the earth and all that springs from it; and for the mystery of life and growth.

We pray that our gratitude may be shown by our care to conserve the powers of the soil, by our readiness to learn from scientific research, and by our concern for a fair distribution of the earth's resources.

We ask these things in the name of Christ our Lord.

Basil Naylor

Men of the sea 353

Your first disciples, Lord, were men of the sea:
    hardy fishermen from the shores of Galilee.
They knew from experience the perils of the deep,
    the stormy wind and the angry waves.
They also knew your presence with them
    in their darkest hours.
We pray for those who face like hazards today
    as sailors and fishermen.
Lord of the sea, be near to guard them
    in every danger, in every need;
and let them hear your voice above the tempest,
    "It is I, be not afraid."
So bring them to their haven in peace,
    for your great mercy's sake.   *Frank Colquhoun*

354

We pray, O God, for all seafarers as they fulfil the duties and face the dangers of their calling:
    the officers and men of the Royal Navy and Merchant Navy;
    the keepers of lighthouses, the crews of lightships and weather-ships, the pilots of our ports;
    all who carry out the services of docks and harbours;

and those who man lifeboats and guard our coasts.

Grant them your strength and protection, and keep them in the hour of special need; for Jesus Christ's sake.

New Every Morning

Scientists **355**

We give thanks, Lord God Almighty,
    for all the advances in knowledge in our day
    and for the benefits of scientific research.
We pray for those engaged in this work,
    and especially in the growth of nuclear science;
and we ask that atomic power and experiment
    may be so wisely controlled by the nations
that its use may always be for peace
    and the furtherance of good in men's lives.
We ask this in the name of Christ our Lord.

Adapted

356

Almighty God, Creator and Lord of all things, we praise you for the knowledge given to men to search out and harness the hidden forces of the world.

Give them also the wisdom and the sense of responsibility to use their knowledge aright, that all research may be employed not for destruction but for the benefit of mankind; through Jesus Christ our Lord. *Adapted*

Use of science **357**

Lord, we have found out so much knowledge
    and yet possess so little wisdom.
We pray that in your mercy
    you will save us from ourselves.
Help us to learn the right use of nature
    no less quickly than we unlock her treasures;

and give us hearts and wills made new in Christ
  to dedicate your gifts of knowledge
to the service of others
  and to the praise of your name.

Timothy Dudley-Smith

Professional sport 358

We pray, O God, for those who engage in sports and contests, for their own pleasure and the entertainment of others.

We ask that through their knowledge of the rules of the game they may see that there are greater laws;

that through their experience of training they may see that there is a greater discipline;

and that through their desire for victory they may be directed to the greatest triumph of all, and the goal which is Christ, the Saviour of the world. For his name's sake. *Christopher Idle*★

359

We pray, Lord, for all engaged in professional sport.

Help them to see their work as part of a wider life, and to remember that all life comes from you.

May they set for themselves the highest standards of personal and professional behaviour, both on the field and off, and provide a wholesome example to those who follow their fortunes; through Jesus Christ our Lord. *Dick Williams*★

Our daily work 360

Help us, O God, to carry into our daily work
  your care for every part of human life,
  a genuine interest in every person with whom we have to do,
  and our calling as men and women commanded to shine as
    lights in the world.
We ask this in Christ's name. *Basil Naylor*

Travellers   **361**

We commend to your keeping, our Father, those who travel
by land or sea or air.

Give them your protection on the way,
enfold them in your peace,

and bring them safely to their journey's end; through Jesus
Christ our Lord.   *New Every Morning*

Those who use the roads   **362**

Lord Jesus Christ, who travelled the roads of Palestine to make
known the gospel of the kingdom, and who finally took the road
that led to the cross: grant to us who use the roads such consideration for others as befits your servants, and such a sense of your will
and direction that we may journey always in faith and hope, for
your great glory.   *Llewellyn Cumings*

363

O God our Father, give to us and to all who use the roads
watchfulness and care and consideration for others; that death
and injury may be caused to none, and all who travel may complete their journey in safety and peace; through Jesus Christ our
Lord.   *Frank M. Best**

The local community **364**

Lᴏʀᴅ of all grace and truth, who came to dwell among men in your own town of Nazareth, we pray that you will give us grace to live in our local community as salt to purify it, and as light to reveal your truth.

May we not be ashamed to acknowledge you as our Saviour; and may we learn so to love and honour all men that peace and goodwill may prevail among us; for your name's sake.

Michael Botting

365

Lord God, you have taught us
    that we are members one of another
    and that none of us lives to himself alone:
we thank you for the community of which we are part;
    for those who share with us in its activities,
    and for all who serve its varied interests.
Help us, as we have opportunity,
    to make our own contribution to the community
    and to learn to be good neighbours,
that by love we may serve one another;
    for the sake of Jesus Christ our Lord.   *Frank Colquhoun*

Civic authorities **366**

Almighty God, from whom comes every good and perfect gift, grant to those who hold office in this *borough* the spirit of justice and truth, of wisdom and charity; that mindful of their responsibility and of the needs of those they serve, they may promote the true welfare of your people and advance your kingdom on earth; through Jesus Christ our Lord.   *Adapted*

367

We pray, O God, for those who hold office in the life of this *borough*, and for all who in various ways serve the community; that fulfilling their duties with singleness of purpose, they may wisely and faithfully exercise the authority committed to them and promote the common good; through Jesus Christ our Lord. *Frank Colquhoun*

See also *676*

Town planners **368**

O God, you have prepared for the redeemed a city not made with hands, radiant with glory, eternal in the heavens: grant to all concerned with the planning of our towns such a vision of order and beauty that the health and welfare of all our citizens may be promoted, and the needs of young and old alike may be supplied; through Jesus Christ our Lord. *Llewellyn Cumings*

A new housing estate **369**

O Lord Christ, who entered the homes of all who were willing to receive you, and so brought the kingdom of God near to them:

send your blessing on us who seek to share the gospel with families on the new housing estate(s) in this area.

Guide us to the sons of peace who will receive your word and your salvation, and grant that from their homes the light of your love may shine out to friends and neighbours.

We ask this for your name's sake. *Llewellyn Cumings,*
Based on Luke 10. 1–12

Social workers **370**

Heavenly Father, whose Son visited mankind in all its suffering and need, and went about doing good: inspire with your love and compassion those engaged in social work in this town [*or* district].

Encourage them when the tasks seem overwhelming.

Give them wisdom when situations seem insoluble.

Challenge them when they are tempted to pass by on the other side.

And help them to show their love for you by their love for their neighbour.

Through Jesus Christ our Lord.   *Michael Botting*

371

We thank you, O God, for those who work in the social services of our country, and here in our own community.

Be with them in their efforts to mend broken lives and broken homes, to help alcoholics and drug addicts, to minister to people in trouble and despair; and give them in their work all needful patience, sympathy and understanding.

We ask it in the name of Jesus Christ our Saviour.   *Adapted*

Family life **372**

O God, the Father of all the families on earth, by the presence of your Holy Spirit protect our families from all evil and strengthen us in what is good.

Enable husbands and wives to live together in mutual consideration, forgiveness and love, under the headship of Christ.

Grant to parents such heavenly wisdom as will enable them to give their children the correction and instruction that belong to a Christian upbringing;

and to children give the desire to grow in wisdom, in stature, and in the knowledge and love of Jesus Christ our Saviour.

Llewellyn Cumings

373

Father in heaven, pattern of all parenthood and lover of children, we pray for homes and families across the world [*or* in this community].

Sustain and comfort them in need and sorrow.

In times of bitterness, tension and division, draw near to heal.

May parents and children together be learners in the school of Christ, daily increasing in mutual respect and understanding, in tolerance and patience, and in all-prevailing love; through Jesus Christ our Lord. *Timothy Dudley-Smith*

374

Father of all, accept our thanks for the joys of family life.

Help us to live so that we may strengthen and enrich the life of the family.

Help us to build with you the kind of family which welcomes the stranger, the lonely and the needy.

Teach us through this small family to love the family of all mankind and to realize our part in it.

In the name of Christ we ask this.

Brother John Charles, SSF

375

Heavenly Father, we bring to you in our prayers
    all whom we love in our family circle,
knowing that your love for them
    is so much greater than ours,
and that your will for them
    is all that is for their good.
So have them in your keeping, O Lord,
    and give them now and always
    the fullness of your blessing;
for Jesus Christ's sake. *Frank Colquhoun*

376

God our Father, be with us in our homes through this and every day.

Help us, when we are tired, to control our wills and tempers and to take thought for others.

Make us loving and patient, forgiving others as we hope to be forgiven; that in our homes your royal law of love may reign; through Jesus Christ our Lord.   *New Every Morning*

Friends   **377**

We thank you, God our Father,
   for the gift of human friendship
and for all the joy and enrichment
   it brings to our lives.
Strengthen our love for our friends,
   and deepen our understanding of their needs;
that we may grow more worthy of that perfect friendship
   which your Son offers to those who do your will;
for your great love's sake.   *Basil Naylor*

The lonely   **378**

We bring to you in our prayers, heavenly Father, all lonely people, especially those who are too old or infirm to enjoy company, and those who are isolated from others through suffering and illness, or through a sense of inferiority.

We pray that friends or neighbours may be enabled to reach them and lift them out of their loneliness and bring them comfort and hope. We ask it in Christ's name.   *Basil Naylor*

379

O God of love,
   present in all places and at all times,
pour your Spirit of healing and comfort
   on every lonely heart.
Have pity on those bereft of human love,

and on those to whom love has never come.
Be to them a strong consolation,
an ever-present help;
and in the end give them fullness of joy,
for the sake of Jesus Christ our Lord.   *Adapted*

The aged   380

Eternal God, we rejoice in your promise
that as our day is, so shall our strength be;
and we ask your help for all who are old
and wearied with the burden of life.
In your strength may they find courage and peace;
and in their advancing years
may they learn more of your love;
through Jesus Christ our Lord.   *James M. Todd*

381

O God our Father, the Creator of the ends of the earth, who
faints not nor grows weary, and whose word abides for ever: be
with all for whom old age brings weariness and weakness.

Support them by your grace, and encourage them with the
assurance of your unfailing love, the sureness of your promises
to all who believe, and the certainty of their inheritance in the
home you have prepared in heaven; through Jesus Christ our
Lord.   *Llewellyn Cumings*

382

Grant, O Lord, that the years that are left may be the holiest,
the most loving, the most mature.

We thank you for the past, and especially that you have kept
the good wine until now.

Help us to accept diminishing powers as the opportunity to
prepare our souls for the full and free life to come in the state
prepared by your Son, Jesus Christ our Lord.

George Appleton

Schools and colleges   **383**

W<small>E</small> offer this prayer, Father, for our schools and colleges:
that those who teach in them may be endowed with the
love and understanding we see revealed in the life and example of
Jesus Christ;

that children may be guided in the way that leads to the abundant life which Jesus came to bring us all;

that students may accept with gratitude and humility your
gifts of mind and the opportunity to use them;

and that the Spirit of truth may use their studies to enlarge
their understanding of your purpose for mankind, made known
in Jesus Christ our Lord.   *Basil Naylor*

384

Almighty God, you are the source of truth
and your Spirit leads us into the truth:
may all who teach and all who learn
in our schools, colleges and universities
be set free from everything that might hinder
their search for the truth;
and finding truth, may they learn to use it
for the good of mankind
and for your greater glory.   *James M. Todd*

385

Almighty God, you have commanded us to love you with all
our mind: help us to grow in knowledge and to be mature in our
thinking, remembering that reverence for you is the beginning
of wisdom.

Bless the work of universities and colleges of education, that in them your name may be honoured and from them may come men and women concerned to know and teach the truth as it is revealed in your Son, Jesus Christ our Lord.   *Michael Botting*

Teachers   386

O Lord our God, in whom are hid all the treasures of wisdom and knowledge, we pray for all who are engaged in the work of education as teachers in our schools, colleges and universities.

Inspire them in their studies to seek and to love the truth, and enable them with joy and patience to share it with others.

Grant above all that they may know that the fear of the Lord is the beginning of wisdom.

This we ask through Jesus Christ our Saviour.

Scripture Union Prayers★

387

Almighty Father, the only wise God,
    source of all grace and truth,
enlighten the minds of those who teach the young
    in the schools of this parish.
Give them understanding of their task
    and a true love for those they serve;
and help them both in their lives
    and by their teaching
to set forward the cause of true religion
    and sound learning;
through Jesus Christ our Lord.   *Frank Colquhoun*

388

Spirit of truth and love, make us apt to teach, but yet more apt to learn; that we may not only desire to share with others what you have revealed to us, but with humble and thankful hearts may always be ready to receive what they have to impart to us; through Jesus Christ our Lord.   *Response*

Children at school 389

O God our Father, we pray for the children growing up in our schools as they prepare for their tasks in life.

May they learn the lessons of greatest worth: self-discipline, integrity of character, care for others, and a true sense of values.

So may they acquire wisdom as well as knowledge, and be strong in spirit to serve their generation and to further your will; through Jesus Christ our Lord. *Frank Colquhoun*

School leavers 390

God of love, we pray for young people who are now leaving school to enter upon the wider life of the world.

As they face the future and all that it holds for them, give them the confidence that their times are in your hands.

Help them to discover your purpose for their lives, that they may find their true fulfilment in your service; through Jesus Christ our Lord. *Frank Colquhoun*

Students from overseas 391

Father of all mankind, bless and guide those who come from overseas to study in our land.

Grant that they may find a welcome and friendship in our homes, colleges and churches; and enable them in the days to come to use their knowledge and skill for the benefit of their own peoples.

We ask it in the name of him in whom all are one, your Son Jesus Christ our Lord.

The rising generation 392

Eternal God, we thank you for our teenage years with all their opportunities of enjoying new experiences, discovering new truths, and developing new powers of body and mind and spirit.

Help us always to remember you, our heavenly Father, and to keep our lives pure by guarding them according to your Word, that we may serve you to the best of our powers all our days, for Jesus' sake. *Michael Botting*

393

Lord, for the vision of youth,
    its love of justice,
    strength of purpose,
    and honesty of mind,
we bring our thanks and praise.
Make plain your living word
    to the rising generation,
that they may grow up in the faith of Christ
    to love and honour your name,
    and to render service to others.
Timothy Dudley-Smith

394

Lord of all life, we pray that as the young people in each new generation discover your world in their own way, their energies may be used creatively in your service, and their choices based on what is true and of real value. We ask it in the name and for the honour of Jesus Christ our Saviour. *Christopher Idle*

THE ARTS

The consecration of art   **395**

G OD of all grace, we thank you for the skills you have given to men, so that through the arts [especially through music, *or* literature, *or* drama] our lives may be inspired and uplifted.

Grant that those who create such works, and we who appreciate them, may be concerned only with what is true, noble, pure, lovely and gracious, so that all artistic expression may direct us to the fullness of truth and beauty as revealed in Jesus Christ your Son our Lord.   *Michael Botting*

396

We thank you, O God, for all your wonderful works,
   and for the creative gifts you have given to men.
We offer our praise, in humility and gladness,
   for all who use these gifts to increase the richness of life;
   for the consecration of art to your service;
   and for all things that help us to see the true nature of your
     creation;
through Jesus Christ our Lord.
        Society of St. Luke the Painter

Artists and craftsmen   **397**

O God, whose Spirit in our hearts teaches us to desire your perfection, to seek for truth and to rejoice in beauty: enlighten and inspire all artists and craftsmen in whatever is true, pure and lovely, that yout name may be honoured and your will done on earth; through Jesus Christ our Lord.
        Society of St. Luke the Painter

Artists and musicians **398**

We thank you, our Father, for the skills of artists and musicians, and for every means by which our life and worship are enriched. Help us to be good stewards of your gifts by using them always in service to you and to one another, for the honour and glory of your name. *Basil Naylor*

Music and musicians **399**

Eternal Lord God, source of all beauty and harmony, we praise you for the gift of music:
for the inspiration given to those who compose it,
for the skill and devotion of those who perform it,
for the faculties and powers which enable us to enjoy it;
and we pray that as by this gift our lives are enriched and renewed, so we may glorify you in a fuller dedication of ourselves, giving thanks always for all things in the name of our Lord Jesus Christ. *Frank Colquhoun*

400

God of creation, you have made all things well
and given us much to enjoy:
we thank you for the gift of music,
through which, far beyond words,
we can feel our way towards the greater mysteries.
We thank you for the skill and sensitivity
of those who by making music
can give such great pleasure;
and we pray that each of us
may be helped to develop those talents
which can be used to benefit others;
through Jesus Christ our Lord. *Roger Pickering*

Writers and readers 401

Christ our Lord, teacher of all truth, raise up in this our day Christian writers who shall be able to communicate the message of the everlasting gospel to men with clarity and conviction.

And to us give grace to take care what we read, and how we read, and above all to hold fast by the words of holy scripture, and by you, Lord Jesus, the Word incarnate, our God for ever and ever. *After Charles Kingsley*

402

Father, we thank you that you have spoken to us through the words of scripture, and chiefly through him who is the living Word of God.

We pray for all who, by what they say and write, influence the lives of others; for those whose daily task is in the use of words.

We ask for them reverence for the truth, sensitiveness to human need, and a true concern for the welfare of the community; through Jesus Christ our Lord. *Basil Naylor*

The theatre 403

O God, the King of glory, who in the making of man bestowed on him the gift of tears and the sense of joy, and implanted in his nature the need for recreation of mind and body: give to those who minister to that need, through drama and music, in the calling of the theatrical profession, a high ideal, a pure intention, and a due sense of responsibility; that their gifts may be used for the enrichment of human character and for your greater glory; through Jesus Christ our Lord.

*Actors' Church Union**

404

Almighty God, giver of all that is good, we thank you for the pleasure and inspiration we derive from the world of drama.

We pray for playwrights and producers, actors and actresses, and all connected with the theatre; that mindful of the influence they exercise in the lives of others they may do their work with a view to promoting man's true enjoyment, and deepening in him a wholesome outlook upon life; through Jesus Christ our Lord.

David Hill

PEOPLE IN NEED

FOR those in need, O Lord, we make our prayer:
  the sick in mind or body,
  the blind and the deaf,
  the fatherless and the widow,
  the sorrowing, the anxious and the perplexed.
Give them courage, patience, and peace of heart, and do for
them whatever is for their good; for the sake of Jesus Christ our
Lord.   *Frank Colquhoun*

406

Our heavenly Father, we commend to your mercy those for
whom life does not spell freedom:
  prisoners of conscience,
  the homeless and the handicapped,
  the sick in body and mind,
  the elderly who are confined to their homes,
  those who are enslaved by their passions,
  and those who are addicted to drugs.
Grant that, whatever their outward circumstances, they may
find inward freedom, through him who proclaimed release to
captives, Jesus Christ our Saviour.   *John R. W. Stott*

407

    Loving Father, we pray for all
    who are any way troubled at this time,
    and especially for those known to us.
    Give relief to those in pain,

friendship to those who are alone,
reassurance to those in doubt or distress of mind;
and may our love be so strong that seeing need
we may never pass by on the other side.
We ask it in Christ's name. *Roger Pickering*

408

To your keeping, O Lord God,
we commend all whose enjoyment of life
has been taken away by sickness,
by tragedy, or by the sin of man.
May your love sustain them in their suffering,
and may your people care for them
in the name of Jesus Christ our Lord.

Roger Pickering

409

Look in your mercy, O Lord our God,
upon the suffering of your world,
and help those in trouble or distress,
whether in mind or in body.
And may our prayer not be made empty by our neglect
but carry with it our readiness
to act as your servants;
that the lonely and the sick,
the anxious and the sorrowing whom we meet
may find us eager to help,
for the sake of Jesus Christ our Lord. *Roger Pickering*

410

Lord Christ, shine upon all who are in the darkness of suffering
or grief; that in your light they may receive hope and courage,
and in your presence may find their rest and peace; for your
love's sake. *Alan Warren*

411

O God of love, we commend to your merciful care and healing grace those whom we have now remembered in our hearts; and we ask you to do for them all that is best, according to their need and according to your will; for the sake of Jesus Christ our Lord. *Frank Colquhoun*

412

Almighty God, in the name of Jesus your Son,
    who healed the sick and consoled the sad,
we pray for all who suffer
    through sickness of body or mind,
    through fear or depression,
    through loneliness or bereavement;
and we ask that according to your will
    they may be healed and comforted,
for the sake of Jesus Christ our Lord. *James M. Todd*

For the aged, see 380–2

Handicapped people
413

Hear our prayer, O God our Father, for those who are called upon to bear the burden of some bodily handicap as they journey through life.

Give them courage to accept the things they cannot change and to face life with brave and trustful hearts, knowing that in their affliction and frustration they are not alone but are surrounded by your love in Jesus Christ our Lord. *Prayers at School**

The underprivileged
414

Forgive us, Father, that we are so eager to make our own lives comfortable whilst others must suffer hunger and want.

Bless the little which we have done and multiply it, in your mercy, to serve the needs of many unknown to us, but known and loved by you; through Jesus Christ our Lord. *Ian D. Bunting*

415

Grant to your afflicted children, Lord God, patience and courage under their sufferings, with hope and peace in their hearts; and grant to us who have enough of this world's goods, so to share our substance and use our skills, that in our day and age we may see all men enter fully into the inheritance which is their birthright; through Jesus Christ our Lord.

*Dick Williams**

416

God of all beauty, whose will it is that all your creatures should enjoy the world and the life you have given us: we know that many are unable to do this, through hunger, poverty, disease, oppression, ignorance, or sin.

Let us never rest content in your joys until we have done everything in our power and by your grace to help others to share them also, O God of all goodness and willer of abundant life; through Jesus Christ our Lord. *George Appleton*

417

God our Father, whose Son Jesus Christ looked with compassion on the hungry people of his day and fed them: hear us as we pray in his name for the starving and undernourished peoples of our world.

Show us, who have so much, what we can do to help those who have so little; and guide and prosper the efforts of those who plan relief and are giving aid, that out of your bounty to mankind the needs of all may be supplied. *Frank Colquhoun*

418

O God our Father, in the name of him who gave bread to the hungry we remember all who, through our human ignorance, folly, selfishness and sin, are condemned to live in want; and we pray that all endeavours for the overcoming of world poverty and hunger may be so prospered that there may be found food sufficient for all. We ask this through Jesus Christ our Lord.

Christian Aid

419

O Lord, we know that we live in a world of plenty, with food sufficient for all.

Help us to realize that there is enough for everyone's need, but not enough for everyone's greed.

Give us hearts of compassion, unselfish concern and loving care, that all may have the abundant life which is your will, O Lord of the hungry crowd and of the twelve basketsful left over.

George Appleton

See also *183*

Christian Aid **420**

Heavenly Father, from whose word we learn that by bearing one another's burdens we can fulfil the law of Christ: we pray that through the work of Christian Aid we may bring comfort, hope and help to those whose needs are so much greater than our own.

Give us the generous love of him who, though he was rich, became poor for us and for our salvation; and move the hearts of all who have it in their power to help to give gladly and freely for his sake, who gave himself to the uttermost for us, even Jesus Christ our Lord. *Christian Aid*

The bereaved **421**

Almighty God, Lord of life and vanquisher of death, we praise you for the sure and certain hope of eternal life which you have given us in the resurrection of our Lord Jesus Christ; and we pray that all who mourn the loss of those dear to them may enter into his victory and know his peace; for his name's sake.

Frank Colquhoun

422

God of love, look mercifully upon those who are now facing the bitterness of bereavement, and give them your peace.

Help them to tread the lonely path before them with faith and courage; and strengthen their hope in him who overcame death and opened for us the gate of life, your Son our Saviour Jesus Christ.

Frank Colquhoun

423

God of hope and giver of all comfort, we commend to your keeping those who mourn the loss of loved ones [and especially those for whom we have been asked to pray].

Give them the peace that passes all understanding, and make them to know that neither death nor life can separate them from your love in Jesus Christ our Lord.

Frank Colquhoun

424

We remember, Lord, the slenderness of the thread which separates life from death,(and the suddenness with which it can be broken.)

Help us also to remember that on both sides of that division we are surrounded by your love.

Persuade our hearts that when our dear ones die neither we nor they are parted from you.

In you may we find peace, and in you be united with them in the body of Christ, who has burst the bonds of death and is alive for evermore, our Saviour and theirs for ever and ever.

Dick Williams

See also 635–8

Those in despair 425

Almighty God, who raised our Lord Jesus Christ from the dead and gave him glory, that we might have hope: have mercy on all in despair, for whom life has lost its meaning and for whom hope has become extinct.

Come to them in pity and power to renew their faith; and enable them to honour you by believing you are able to make all things new, through Jesus Christ our Lord.

Llewellyn Cumings

Those who doubt 426

Most merciful God, we pray
    for those who doubt your love;
      for those who find it difficult to believe or to pray;
      for those who have lost a faith they once possessed.
May the Holy Spirit enlighten their minds
    and lead them into all truth,
through Jesus Christ our Lord.   *Frank Colquhoun*

427

Lord Jesus, Son of Man, you know the struggle of the human mind in its search for truth.

Give courage to those who wrestle with their uncertainties;

save them from an easy and uncritical acceptance of other men's beliefs;

and uphold them with your loving Spirit through their experience of darkness till they reach the light of honest conviction; for the honour of your name.   *Basil Naylor*

Those in prison 428

Most gracious Jesus, our Lord and our God, who bore our sins in your own body on the tree: remember in your mercy all those who are under sentence of punishment in our prisons; that by true repentance and your gracious pardon they may be saved in the day of your coming; and to all governors, chaplains, warders and visitors, grant patience and sympathy, forbearance and understanding; for your tender mercy's sake.   *A. E. Long*

429

We pray, our Father, for those whose freedom has been taken from them:

for all who suffer imprisonment, whether for crime or for conscience sake;

for all whose vision of your world is seen through bars, and in whose heart the lamp of hope burns low.

God of mercy, give them help, according to their need, and hear our prayer for Jesus Christ's sake.   *Timothy Dudley-Smith*

430

Heavenly Father, whose Son came to redeem mankind and to be the friend of sinners: we commend to your mercy those who have offended against the law and are serving prison sentences.

Make known to them your unchanging love; turn their hearts to yourself in true repentance; and give them renewal of hope and the opportunity of making a fresh beginning; for the sake of Jesus Christ our Lord.   *Frank Colquhoun*

The unchanging Christ   431

Lord Christ, when you were here on earth
you stilled the storm, fed the hungry,
healed the sick and cast out demons.
You are the same yesterday, today, and for ever.
So make known to us now, O Lord, your grace and power.
Speak to our restless hearts your word of peace.
Satisfy the hunger of our souls.
Make our lives whole and strong,
and rescue us from the power of evil;
for the glory of your great name.   *Frank Colquhoun*

SICKNESS AND HEALTH

The ministry of healing **432**

OUR Father, whose Son came to bring wholeness to the lives of men: we thank you for the wealth of knowledge brought to us through medical research, and for the healing ministry of doctors, surgeons and nurses.

We pray that all who work in different ways for the health of their fellow men may be brought into unity of purpose and learn to co-operate with one another, in the spirit of him who is the perfect and whole Man, Jesus Christ our Lord.   *Basil Naylor*

433

God of all grace, we ask your blessing on the work of doctors, nurses and those who tend the sick, especially in the hospitals of this town [*or* city, neighbourhood].

Strengthen them for their tasks, and give them the joy of knowing that they are instruments in fulfilling your own purpose of healing, in Jesus Christ our Lord.   *Adapted*

434

God of love, giver of life and health,
    we pray for all who in their various callings
serve the needs of men and women
    in sickness of body or mind.
Equip them as your fellow workers
    in the ministry of healing,
and strengthen them to share in the task
    of making life whole;
through Jesus Christ our Lord.   *Basil Naylor*

435

Bless, O Lord Christ, all whom you have called to share in your own ministry of healing as doctors and nurses. Give them skill, understanding and compassion, and enable them to do their work in dependance on your grace and for the promotion of your glory. *Adapted*

Hospitals

436

O God, the Father of mankind, to whom alone is known the mystery of suffering, hear our prayers on behalf of those in hospital who are bearing the burden of sickness or pain, or have to undergo an operation.

In their weakness and anxiety draw near to them with your comfort and strength, and give them the assurance that, sharing their suffering, you will also share with them your peace, in Jesus Christ our Lord. *Prayers for Use in Hospitals**

437

Lord Jesus Christ, who in the days of your life here on earth showed compassion to the sick and afflicted and made them whole: bless those who are carrying on your healing work in our hospitals and nursing homes.

Give them sympathy and skill, and an ever deepening understanding of their task; that in your mercy those who suffer in body or mind may be restored to fullness of health. We ask it for your name's sake. *Frank Colquhoun*

The sick

438

Almighty God, whose Son our Lord Jesus Christ was made perfect by the things that he suffered: have compassion on those who are passing through illness and pain. Uphold their faith, that they may trust and not be afraid; and give them the comfort and strength of your presence, for your tender mercy's sake.

Adapted

439

Lord Jesus Christ, in the days of your flesh
    the sick were brought to you for healing:
hear us as we now bring to you in our prayers
    those who are ill, in body or in mind.
May your presence be with them
    to relieve suffering and distress
and to restore them to fullness of life,
    for your great love's sake.   *Frank Colquhoun*

440

Remember in mercy, our Father, those who are passing through illness, and especially those of whom we are now thinking in our prayers . . .

Bless all that is being done for their good, and surround them with your healing love and power, for the sake of Jesus Christ our Saviour.   *Frank Colquhoun*

441

Father, we bring to you in the name of our Lord Jesus Christ those whose lives are broken by ill-health. May your healing Spirit assist all who work to restore them, that in your goodness they may find wholeness in body, mind and spirit, for the glory of your name.

442

God of all grace, we pray that those who suffer physical pain or mental distress may find your presence near them, and in your mercy they may be restored to health of body and mind.

We ask it in the name of him who both suffered for us and healed the sufferings of others, your Son our Saviour Jesus Christ.
    Adapted

The mentally ill   **443**

Lord Jesus Christ, who for love of our souls entered the deep
darkness of the cross: we pray that your love may surround all
who are in the darkness of great mental distress and who find it
difficult to pray for themselves.

May they know that darkness and light are both alike to you
and that you have promised never to fail them or forsake them.

We ask it for your name's sake.   *Llewellyn Cumings*

444

O God, the maker of men's minds and healer of their ills: bless
all your children who suffer from mental distress.

Help them to trust you even on the darkest days, and to know
that you are with them in their deepest need; and in your mercy
release them from the cause of their sickness, that they may love
and serve you with all their strength and with all their mind;
through Jesus Christ our Lord.   *Dick Williams*

445

Father, we pray for the mentally ill,
   for all who are of a disturbed and troubled mind.
Be to them light in their darkness,
   their refuge and strength in time of fear.
Give special skills and tender hearts
   to all who care for them,
and show them how best to assist your work of healing;
   through Jesus Christ our Lord.   *Timothy Dudley-Smith*

446

Lord Jesus Christ, you healed many who were mentally ill,
and in your name we pray for a deeper understanding of those
whose minds are disturbed.

Give knowledge and skill to those who treat them, patience and kindness to those who nurse them; and draw together in a closer fellowship of healing all who are working to further your will by making men whole.   *Basil Naylor*

447

Most merciful Father, we bring to you in our prayers
    those suffering from mental strain and sickness,
    especially those whom we remember in our hearts.
Give them, now and always,
    the assurance of your unchanging love;
and make your presence real to them,
    that they may trust and not be afraid.
So may they find peace, O God,
    and healing of the mind,
through our Lord and Saviour Jesus Christ.

Frank Colquhoun

The incurable   **448**

We commend to your mercy, O God, those who are suffering from illnesses which are beyond the reach of human skill.

Give them courage to endure patiently, and faith to trust you fully, even though your way is hidden from their sight.

So may they fear no evil, knowing that you are with them, and will be with them to the end; through Jesus Christ our Lord.

Adapted

449

Almighty God, whose grace is sufficient
    for all our need,
and whose power comes to full strength
    in our weakness:
we pray for all who suffer
    and who never get well,

that sustained in their weakness
    and released from pain,
they may rejoice in the power of Christ
    resting upon them.
We ask this in his name.   *James M. Todd*

Medical research 450

God of all grace, you have taught us in your Word that the leaves of the tree of life are for the healing of the nations, and that every accursed thing shall be banished in the age to come: have regard to the sufferings of humanity, and grant such success to all engaged in medical research that their work may be used to alleviate pain and to further the ministry of healing among people of every nation; for the sake of Jesus Christ our Lord.

Llewellyn Cumings

Drug addicts 451

O Lord Jesus Christ, who came not to condemn but to save men: look in mercy on those who are in the grip of drugs.

Release them from the captivity into which their own actions have brought them;

    give them the will to accept a cure where such is possible;

    and restore to them the possibility of a new life, through the grace and power of our Lord Jesus Christ.   *Andrew Warner*

452

Almighty Father, whose blessed Son refused at Calvary the deadening wine: have pity on all who seek unlawful escape from their sorrows, and by the virtue of his cross give them grace to share his passion and his victory; who with the Comforter and you reigns triumphant in eternal joy.   *Henry Cooper*

Alcoholics 453

O loving Saviour, who consecrates the fruit of the vine in the mystery of the eucharist: give grace to all who degrade their persons by drinking to excess; and control and consecrate their lives to your service; through the merits of your fasting and temptation, and in union with the Father and the Holy Spirit.

Henry Cooper

The dying 454

We pray, gracious Father, for those whose earthly life is drawing to its close, that you will grant to them the comfort of your presence.

Relieve all distress, remove every fear, and give peace now and at the last, through Jesus Christ our Lord.

Frank Colquhoun

The gift of health 455

Make us always thankful, our heavenly Father,
    for your most precious gift of health;
for our sight, our speech, our hearing;
    for all the powers of body and mind
    which enable us to enjoy life to the full.
Teach us to safeguard the health that is ours;
    deepen our compassion for those who suffer illness;
and help us to use the days of our strength
    in your service and for your glory;
through Jesus Christ our Lord.   *Frank Colquhoun*

THE CHURCH: MISSION AND SERVICE

An act of penitence **456**

FATHER, forgive the apathy and cowardice which hamper
our witness as Christians;

our busy occupation with lesser things which prevents us from
seeing the great vision of your kingdom on earth;

our pride and jealousy which keep us from involvement with
others in your service;

our many failures to mould our desires and plans into the
shape of your loving will;

our prejudices which hold us back from doing what you have
called us to do in the mission of your Church;

our unreasoned fear of change and of new patterns of unity
in ministry and worship;

our little faith; our loss of hope; our lack of love.

Father, forgive what we have been;
inspire what we are;
and direct what we shall be;
through Jesus Christ our Lord. *Warwickshire Prayer Card*

An act of thanksgiving **457**

Father, we thank you

for the gift of Jesus Christ to be the Way, the Truth, and the
Life;

for the love which moved him to endure the cross for us and
for all mankind;

for the victory of his resurrection and the glory of his ascension;

for the outpouring of the Holy Spirit and the witness of the
Church through many centuries;

for the encouragement of our growing awareness that we are
all one in Christ Jesus;

for the blessings received in belonging to each other in the
fellowship of the Holy Spirit;

for the privilege of being called to discipleship of Jesus Christ,
to bear witness to his eternal presence and his saving power.

For all these joyful gifts, thanks be to you, O God.

Warwickshire Prayer Card

World mission 458

We pray, O God, for the Church in the world of today:

that it may be true to its gospel and responsive to the needs of
mankind;

that it may conserve what is good in the past and reach out
boldly to the future;

that it may care for the individual and help to change society;

and that it may have a growing unity without sacrificing all
variety of response to your grace.

We ask it in the name of Jesus Christ our Lord.

Roger Tomes

459

Almighty God, you have called your Church
to share in your mission to the whole world:
give to us and to all your people
such belief in the gospel
and such faithfulness in service
that the life of mankind may be renewed
in the knowledge and love of your Son,
Jesus Christ our Lord.   *James M. Todd*

460

We pray, O God, for your Church throughout the world, that Christians may respond wholeheartedly to your love by committing themselves to the service of your kingdom, with faith strengthened by a living experience of Christ's presence, and with freedom and courage to follow where Christ leads, for the honour of his name.   *Church Missionary Society*

461

Lord, you have consecrated the world
   by sending your Son into the midst of it
   and by making all things new in him.
We ask you to give us and all your people
   the courage and power we need
   to share fully in his mission to the world
and to further his kingdom in the lives of men,
   to the honour and glory of his name.
                    Church Missionary Society

462

O God, you have called men and women of every land to be a holy nation, a royal priesthood, the Church of your dear Son: unite us in mutual love across the barriers of race and culture, and strengthen us in our common task of being Christ and showing Christ to the world he came to save.   *John Kingsnorth*

463

Give your grace, O Lord our God,
   to the Church of Jesus Christ in every land;
that in fulfilling its apostolic mission
   it may be faithful in the preaching of the gospel,
   compassionate in its concern for the suffering,
   and courageous in its testimony for truth and righteousness;
for the furtherance of your kingdom
   and the glory of your holy name.   *Frank Colquhoun*

Christ's witnesses 464

O God, as those who seek to be your witnesses in a minority situation, where your claims are so largely ignored or denied, we pray that we may bear our Christian witness by what we are and not simply by what we profess or preach.

Give us true holiness of character, a deeper understanding of people and their needs, and a love that is humble, outgoing and open.

So may our lives reflect something of your grace made known to us in Jesus Christ our Lord.

Based on words of George Appleton

465

Father, you have committed to men
   the good news of your saving love
and set us as ambassadors for Christ
   in your world:
help us together to bear witness
   to the message of reconciliation,
that in the life of your Church
   men may become new creatures
   in Jesus Christ our Lord.

Collects with the New Lectionary

466

Eternal God and Father, give to us and to all your people grace and courage to proclaim your mighty work in Christ, in the crib and on the cross and in the world today. May we work together for the coming of the kingdom in our own time, ever looking in joyful hope for its consummation at the end of the age, through Jesus Christ our Lord. *John Kingsnorth*

The Church's ministry of reconciliation **467**

Father, who formed the family of man to live in harmony and peace: we acknowledge before you our divisions, quarrels, hatreds, injustices and greed.

May your Church demonstrate before the world the power of the gospel to destroy divisions, so that in Christ Jesus there may be no barriers of wealth or class, age or intellect, race or colour, but all may be equally your children, members one of another and heirs together of your everlasting kingdom.

Timothy Dudley-Smith

468

Grant, O God, that your Church may increasingly become
a reconciling force among the peoples,
witnessing to the unity of all men
in the family of the one Father;
checking passion in time of strife,
reminding men of the ways of Christ,
and exhibiting above all things
that brotherhood of mankind taught by our Master,
Jesus Christ our Lord. *C. R. Forrester*

469

Lord Christ, who by your cross and passion
    reconciled the world to God
and broke down the barriers of race and colour
    which divide men and nations:
make us and all your people
    instruments of reconciliation in the life of our world,
that we may inherit the blessing
    which you promised to the peacemakers.

Frank Colquhoun

The World Council of Churches 470

Almighty God our heavenly Father, whose Son Jesus Christ has broken down the barriers that divide man from man: we ask you to bless the World Council of Churches, that it may bear true witness to your activity in our midst, give voice to the Christian concern for justice and holiness, and serve the needs of the poor and under-privileged; and hasten the time, O God, when your Church shall be one and be seen to be one; through the same Jesus Christ our Lord. *John Kingsnorth*

Home evangelism 471

Father, you show the world the way to live through the words, life, death and resurrection of your Son Jesus: grant us your grace, that we who follow him may unite to proclaim by word and deed your way to the people of this country; through Jesus Christ our Lord. *Call to the North*

Witness to the Jews 472

O God our Father, we thank you for inspiring Hebrew writers to give us the Bible, and Hebrew prophets to prepare the way of Christ.

We thank you for the Jewish disciples who were the first missionaries and preachers of the good news.

Above all we thank you for Jesus your Son, born of a Jewish mother.

Help us to repay so great a debt by doing all we can to send the message of Jesus Christ back to the Jewish people, that they with us may rejoice in his great salvation.

We ask it for the glory of his name. *Walter Barker★*

473

Almighty God, who in days of old called your servant Abraham to go into an unknown land and promised him that through his family all nations of the earth would find a blessing: we thank you for Jesus the Messiah, in whom this promise came true.

We pray for the Jewish people, Abraham's descendants, who do not know our Saviour. Help all who try to tell them of him, and soon bring them home to your flock under the care of the Good Shepherd, Jesus Christ our Lord.

Walter Barker★

Those of other religions   **474**

Lord of all truth, make us as Christians sensitive and humble in our approach to all men.

As we learn of their search for truth within the terms of other religions, help us also to see your search for them.

Grant that by your Spirit, and through the obedience of your disciples, what they have learned of you and your love may find its fulfilment in Christ, through whom alone we come to the full knowledge of yourself, God blessed for ever.   *Alan Nugent*

475

Word of God and Light of men, we ask you to bless all those of other faiths with whom we share our lives and who serve the needs of our community.

Help us to discern in them the Light that lightens every man, and to love them with a love like yours; that as we join with them in service to others we may be drawn closer to you, the Way, the Truth, and the Life.   *Basil Naylor*

476

Source of all truth and Lord of all life, it was your Son Jesus Christ who taught us to call you Father and to acknowledge that none may come to you except through him.

Enable us to recognize with gratitude those elements of truth and justice in other beliefs.

Encourage us to love and care for those who search for you under other names; but keep us from ever denying the uniqueness of Jesus, and fire us with the desire to make him known as mankind's only Saviour and Lord.   *Michael Saward*

Missionary recruits   477

> Lord God, the harvest is plentiful
>   but the labourers are few.
> And so we pray that you,
>   the Lord of the harvest,
> will send forth labourers into your harvest,
>   to preach the good news to the nations,
>   to build up your Church in every land,
>   and to serve the needs of mankind everywhere;
> for the sake of Jesus our Saviour.   *Frank Colquhoun*

The persecuted church   478

Almighty God, you have called your people to shine as lights in the world; we pray for our fellow Christians who bear their witness in difficult places, and for those who suffer persecution and imprisonment for the gospel's sake.

Uphold their faith; bless their testimony; give them freedom of spirit; and cause your Word everywhere to speed on and triumph, for the honour of our Lord and Saviour Jesus Christ.

Frank Colquhoun

479

Lord God, the refuge and strength of your people in every hour of need: uphold all who suffer for their allegiance to the faith of Christ. Give them courage and patience to endure to the end; and by their example and witness may they win others to the service of him who suffered for all mankind, our Saviour Jesus Christ.   *Worship Now**

The caring church   480

Most merciful Father, you have called us to be a caring church, reflecting in our lives your infinite care for us your children.

Help us to fulfil our calling and to care for one another in an unselfish fellowship of love; and to care for the world around us in sharing with it the good news of your love and serving those who suffer from poverty, hunger and disease.

We ask it in the name of Christ our Lord.

Based on words of Abp. Michael Ramsey

481

O Lord, let the Church be truly your collective body in the world today, the Christ-community directed by you its head, infused with your Spirit, loving and serving men as you did when you lived our human life.

Help the Church to give itself for the world, so that men may have the priceless treasure of your grace and love, O Lord of the Church, O Saviour of the world.   *George Appleton*

The servant church   **482**

Give to your Church, O God, the grace to follow in the steps of Jesus, who came among us as one who serves.

May it be ready in all the world to spend and be spent in the service of the poor and the hungry, the sick and the ignorant.

May it work with strength and suffer with courage for the liberation of the oppressed and the restoration to all men of the dignity and freedom of those created in your image.

Grant this, our Father, for the sake of the same Jesus Christ our Lord.   *John Kingsnorth*

Renewal of the Church   **483**

A WAKEN, O God, your Church throughout the world
     to see in all the tensions and unrest of these times
   the cross of Christ as the one way of peace;
and let the living Spirit of the Lord
   so move among Christian people everywhere
that there may be a revival of that faith
   by which of old the lost were saved,
   the captives were set free,
   men's hearts were changed,
   and righteousness became victorious over sin.
We ask it in the name of our Saviour Jesus Christ.

Prayers of World Fellowship

484

O God, whose matchless power is ever new and ever young:
pour out your Spirit upon us and your whole Church; that with
renewed faith, vision and obedience we may the more joyfully
testify to your new creation in Christ, and more selflessly serve
your new order amidst the old; for the glory of our Lord and
Saviour Jesus Christ.   *Adapted*

485

Lord our God, giver of all grace, have mercy on your Church
throughout the world.
   Renew its life;
   restore its unity;
   sanctify its worship;

empower its witness;

and make it a fit instrument for the furtherance of Christ's kingdom among men, to the glory of his great name.

Frank Colquhoun

486

Guide and direct, O Lord, the minds of all who work for the reshaping of the Church in our time.

Restore our faith and vision.

Renew our energies and love.

Revive your people to new life and power.

So may we live and speak for Christ before the world he came to save, and ever advance his kingdom, for his honour and glory.

Timothy Dudley-Smith

487

Lord God, heavenly Father,
grant to your Church today
   the faith of her apostles,
   the hope of her martyrs,
   and the love of her Lord,
even Jesus Christ, in whose name we pray.

Christopher Idle

488

Eternal God, keep your chosen people
   true to their ancient calling,
   alive to their present opportunity,
   and confident of their glorious inheritance;
through Jesus Christ our Lord.   *Christopher Idle*

489

O God, rouse your Church, lest we sleep and miss men's need of you and your yearning love for men.

O God, cleanse your Church and forgive our lack of zeal for your kingdom.

O God, set your Church ablaze with the fire of your Spirit, that we may spend and be spent for your gospel, your will, and your glory, all our days.

Through Jesus Christ our Lord.   *George Appleton*

The fellowship of the free   490

Build us up, O Father, into the fellowship of the free
that starts in each family and reaches out to the people next door;
that starts in our own congregations and reaches over barriers
    of custom and prejudice to the church down the street;
that starts in our own country and reaches beyond patriotism
    and national pride to the nations of the world;
that starts with our own colour and rejoices to claim as brothers
    men of every race.
Lead us all, O wise and loving Father,
to the kingdom of your dear Son,
    where there is no pain and no fear,
    no hunger and no greed,
    no oppressor and no oppressed,
but all are full-grown men in Christ,
    our only Lord and Saviour.   *John Kingsnorth*

The Church's unity   491

Heavenly Father, in your word you have taught us to maintain the unity of the Spirit in the bond of peace:

forgive our complacency with the present divisions in your Church.

Break down the barriers of pride and misunderstanding which keep us and our fellow Christians apart.

Make us more humble and deepen our love one for another;
and show us how we can more closely worship and work
together as members of the one Body of Christ our Lord.

Frank Colquhoun

492

Holy Father, whose Son our Lord Jesus Christ
    prayed not only for his chosen apostles
but also for those who were to believe in him
    through their word,
      that they all might be one:
look in mercy on the body of the Church
    and heal its divisions;
that its restored life may manifest
    the reconciling power of the gospel,
and the world may believe that you sent your Son
    to be its Saviour.
For his name's sake. *Adapted*

493

Heavenly Father, in whose eyes your Church is one in spite of
human prejudice and sin: give to us your servants
    such penitence for our divisions,
    such love for one another,
    and such devotion to your service,
    that we may find again our unity in your Son Jesus Christ our
Lord. *Sydney Linton**

494

Lord Jesus Christ, you said to your apostles:
I leave you peace, my peace I give you.
Look not on our sins but on the faith of your Church,
and grant us the peace and unity of your kingdom
where you live and reign for ever and ever.

Roman Order of Mass

495

Lord Jesus, the day before you died for us you prayed that your disciples might be one as you are one with the Father.

Help us, divided as we are, to grieve for our unfaithfulness.

Give us the honesty to acknowledge and the courage to reject our apathy, our mistrust, and our intolerance.

Make us one in heart and mind in your love, that being bound together in true fellowship we may present a united witness to the world, according to your will and for the glory of your name.

Adapted

496

Merciful God, in whose Church there is one Lord, one faith, one baptism:

grant us always to acknowledge the lordship of your Son Jesus Christ,

to confess with our whole lives the one true faith,

and to live in love and unity with all who have been baptized in his name;

through the same Jesus Christ, to whom with you, Father, and the Spirit, be glory now and for evermore.   *Worship Now*

497

O God our Father, bless your Church with unity, peace and concord. Make her here and all over the world a true fellowship of the Spirit in which no distinction is made because of race or colour, class or party: a fellowship of love in which all are really one in Christ.

We ask it in his name, who is our one Lord.

*William Barclay**

498

O God, whose will it is that all your children should be one in Christ: we pray for the unity of your Church.

Pardon all our pride and our lack of faith, of understanding and of charity, which are the cause of our divisions.

Deliver us from our narrow-mindedness, from our bitterness, from our prejudices.

Save us from considering as normal that which is a scandal to the world and an offence to your love.

Teach us to recognize the gifts of your grace among all those who call upon you and confess the faith of Jesus Christ our Lord.

*Liturgy of the Reformed Church of France**

499

O Christ, keep us as your servants faithful and active in our quest for that unity in truth and holiness for which you prayed; and draw us closer to one another through being closer to you, that so we may become perfectly one, as you are one with the Father, to the glory of your name. *Based on John 17*

The unity we have **500**

We give thanks, our Father, for the unity
which is already ours as Christians.
We thank you that there is
one Body and one Spirit,
one hope which belongs to our calling,
one Lord, one faith, one baptism,
one God and Father of us all.
And we resolve by your grace that
walking with all lowliness and meekness,
and forbearing one another in love,
we may maintain the unity of the Spirit
in the bond of peace,
through Jesus Christ our Lord.
Based on Ephesians 4. 1–6

Unity in mission 501

Father, we pray for your Church throughout the world, that it may share to the full in the work of your Son, revealing you to men and reconciling men to you and to one another; that we and all Christian people may learn to love one another as you have loved us, and your Church may more and more reflect the unity which is your will and your gift in Jesus Christ our Lord.

Coventry Cathedral

502

Heavenly Father, whose Son prayed that we might be completely one, so that the world would recognize that it was you who sent him:

help us so to open our hearts and minds to the Holy Spirit that we may indeed become one in the mission which you have entrusted to us.

May we be known as true disciples of our Lord, and may many through us be brought to put their trust in him, for the glory of his great name. *Warwickshire Prayer Card*

One holy catholic and apostolic Church 503

Lord of the Church
> make the Church one,
>> and heal our divisions;
> make the Church holy,
>> in all her members and in all her branches;
> make the Church catholic,
>> for all men and in all truth;
> make the Church apostolic,
>> with the faith and mission of the first apostles.
We ask it in the name of Jesus Christ our Lord.

George Appleton

ACTS OF THANKSGIVING

General   **504**

WE give thanks, O God our Father, for the many blessings
of this life:

for health and strength and all our powers of body and mind;

for our homes and loved ones and for the wonderful joy of
friendship;

for our work and the opportunity of service;

for the beauty and bounty of the world of nature;

for the kindness, generosity and sympathy shown to us by so
many along life's journey.

Give us thankful hearts, O God, for all your goodness, and help
us by the way we live to repay some of the debt we owe; for the
sake of him who came not to be served but to serve, your Son
our Saviour Jesus Christ.   *Adapted*

505

O God of love, accept our hearty thanks
    for all that you have given us so richly to enjoy:
for health of mind and body
    when many are sick and afflicted;
for homes, loved ones and friendship
    when many are lonely and desolate;
for sight and hearing
    when many are blind or deaf;
for food and clothing
    when many starve and go in rags;
for security and hope
    when many are anxious and in despair;

and above all for your redeeming love
　　made known to us in Jesus our Saviour.
Help us to show our gratitude
　　by using our lives in your service,
　　and in the service of men;
through Jesus Christ our Lord.　　　　　*Gordon Hyslop*

506

We praise you, God our Father, for the richness of your creation,
　　for the uniqueness of each person,
　　for the creativity which sustains and renews our cultures,
　　for your faithfulness towards your people.
We praise you, Jesus our Lord, for your constant meddling in our
　　affairs,
　　for your identification with the poor,
　　for your sacrifice for all men on the cross,
　　for revealing the true man to all people.
We praise you, God the Spirit, for your inspiration of life,
　　for your insistence to draw us always to Christ,
　　for the infusion of unrest among men,
　　for your patient preparation of the fulfilment of history.
We praise you, blessed Trinity, for not doing for us according to
　　our sins,
　　for continuing your love to all that lives,
　　for continuing your disturbing call to repentance,
　　for continuing life on earth.
　　　　　　　　　WCC Bangkok Conference 1973

507

O God of love, make us more thankful
　　for all the boundless mercies of our daily life.
Forgive us that we are so often ungrateful,
　　complaining and discontented,
taking for granted your greatest gifts:

the blessings of health,
the comforts of home and family life,
the joys of friendship,
and the beauty of the world around us.
Teach us day by day to number our blessings
and to receive each of them as from our Father's hand;
and fill our lives with gratitude,
our lips with praise;
for the sake of Jesus Christ our Lord.   *Frank Colquhoun*

508

O God, our heavenly Father, we acknowledge your love and kindness to us your children: you have given us life and health and every good thing which we enjoy.

We thank you that you have made this world so beautiful and that there is so much in it for us to enjoy, and so many things that enrich our lives.

We thank you for the blessings of home and family life, and for the marvellous gift of friendship.

And in a special way we thank you for your presence with us along life's journey, and for those who on the way have revealed to us the loveliness of Christ and made faith in him a living reality.

Receive our gratitude, O Lord, and make us more worthy of your goodness; for Jesus Christ's sake.

Based on a prayer by G. H. Russell

509

Almighty God, we lift up our hearts in gratitude for all your loving kindness to us your children.
For life and health, for love and friendship, and for the goodness and mercy that have followed us all the days of our life.
For the wonder and beauty of the world; and for all things true and honest, just and pure, lovely and of good report.

For the gift of Jesus Christ your Son; for the grace and truth
which came by him; and for his obedience unto death, even
the death of the cross.

For his glorious resurrection, his ascension to your right hand,
and for his everlasting kingdom and glory.

For the Holy Spirit, the Comforter, the Lord and Lifegiver; for
your holy Church throughout the world; for your Word
and Sacraments and all the means of grace; and for the fellowship of the redeemed in heaven and on earth.

Glory, thanksgiving, and praise be yours, O Father Almighty;
through Jesus Christ our Lord, who is alive and reigns with you
and the Holy Spirit, one God, world without end.

*Book of Common Order**

510

Father, we thank you for all that you have given us.
We thank you
    for the changing beauty of the world,
    the beauties of cloud and sunshine, night and day.
We thank you
    for the talents and powers you have given to men,
    and for all the good use to which these have been put.
We thank you
    for showing your love for us and for all men,
    for teaching us to love each other,
    and for all the love that we receive each day.
Most of all we thank you for Jesus:
    for his life of love,
    for his teaching and example,
    for his death on the cross,
    for the new life he has brought to us,
    and for all that we enjoy because of his perfect love.

Father, Son, and Holy Spirit,
> three persons in one eternity of love,
> we thank you, and will thank you, for ever.

*Worship Now**

For God's revelation   511

We give thanks, O God, for the wonder of your dealings with
men, from the beginning until now:

for your creative word, by which the heavens and the earth were
made;

for making man in your own image, able to hear and answer your
call;

for the written word, which has been a lamp to our feet, and still
shines upon our way;

for the mystery of the Word made flesh in the coming of our
Lord Jesus Christ;

for the preservation of your true and living word in the Church;

for your word to us in these days, calling us to repentance and
assuring us of pardon;

we thank you, O God, and praise your name,
> through our Lord and Saviour Jesus Christ.

New Every Morning

For the Church's witness   512

We thank you, O Lord, for revealing yourself to man, and for
all who have been your messengers in the world:

for the first apostles of Christ, sent out to preach the gospel to
every nation;

for those who brought the good news to our own land;

for all who in ages of darkness shone as lights in the world;

for all your followers in every age who have given their lives for
the faith;

for those in our own day who have gone to the ends of the earth
as heralds of your love;

for the innumerable company who now praise you out of every
    race and nation.
With these and with your whole Church we worship you and
    magnify your holy name.   *New Every Morning*

A brief thanksgiving   **513**

We thank you, Father, for all our joy and all our longing.
You have given us in this world beauty and love;
you have also given us the ordinary, necessary things of daily life.
We thank you, Father, not only for these things
but for the gift of hope,
and for all that reminds us of your promise of eternal life;
through Jesus Christ our Lord.   *Worship Now*

For use at a family service   **514**

Our Lord God, we thank you for all your blessings,
    for life and health,
    for laughter and fun,
    for all our powers of mind and body,
    for our homes and the love of dear ones,
    for everything that is beautiful, good and true.
But above all we thank you for giving your Son
    to be our Saviour and Friend.
May we always find our true happiness in pleasing you
    and helping others to know and love you,
    for Jesus Christ's sake.   *Family Worship*

                            515

We thank you, heavenly Father, for all your goodness to us and
    to all men.
For the world in which you have placed us, with its wonder and
    beauty.
For life and health, for food and clothing, for kind friends and
    happy homes.

For those who love us, and for all who have shown us in their lives a good example.

Most of all, for Jesus Christ, your only Son our Saviour, who came into the world and died for us on the cross, and rose again from the dead, and is now our Friend in heaven.

Glory and honour, dominion and power, be yours, O God, Father, Son and Holy Spirit, for ever and ever.

*Book of Common Order**

For other acts of thanksgiving, see Index

III
PRAYERS FOR PARISH OCCASIONS

THE PARISH

ALMIGHTY God, you have made us members of Christ and of his Church in this parish.

May we as a congregation reach upwards to your throne in worship and adoration; inwards to one another in understanding and fellowship; and outwards to the world in evangelism and social compassion.

Make us like a city set on a hill whose light cannot be hidden, so that men and women may find Christ as the light of the world, and his Church as the family of the redeemed, and eternal life as the gift of God through Jesus Christ our Lord.

Maurice A. P. Wood

517

Prosper with your blessing, O Lord, the work to which you have called us in this parish and strengthen the hands of all who serve you.

Make our worship more worthy, our witness more effective, our lives more holy; and inspire us all with fresh zeal in the furtherance of your kingdom; for the honour of our Lord and Saviour Jesus Christ.   *Frank Colquhoun*

518

God, who made every man
and who may be found in every place:
    make this parish a caring neighbourhood,
    make your people a true community,
    make your Church a living cell of the one body of your Son,
Jesus Christ our Lord.   *Christopher Idle*

519

We pray, our Father, for all the people
 for whom this church is responsible.
We pray that among the homes of the parish,
  its schools and hospitals,
  its shops and offices and factories,
  its streets and parks,
  its places of entertainment
  and its places of worship,
 your name may be hallowed,
 your kingdom come,
 and your will be done;
 through Jesus Christ our Lord.   *Christopher Idle*

520

God bless this church and parish,
 and prosper all our attempts to be faithful
 and to draw others to you,
 for Jesus Christ's sake.

                    From an old Scottish prayer

Intercessions for a parish   **521**

  Let us pray together for the progress of Christ's mission here
in . . . and seek God's guidance and help in the tasks to which
he has called us in this parish. We pray:

  For a growing unity with Christians of other churches and
    denominations in obedience to Christ's will.

  For the church officers and members of the church council in
    their responsibility as leaders in making known the gospel
    of Christ in this neighbourhood.

  For the teaching ministry of this church, that we may be well
    equipped and instructed in the truths of our faith.

  For those who have the care of children and young people, in
    schools and youth organizations.

For those who share in the ministry of care, counsel and comfort, and those to whom they minister: the sick, the sorrowful, the aged, and the lonely.

For our civic leaders and those who maintain the health and safety of the community; for the social services and the industrial life of this town.

For ourselves as church members, that we may have grace to proclaim through our lives the joy of Christ's victory.

Almighty God, as you have called us to serve you here in the mission of the gospel, and in the ministry of your love to all men, so bless us with the wisdom and power of your Spirit, that we may know your will and be strong to obey it, for the honour of our Lord and Saviour Jesus Christ.   *Basil Naylor*

During an interregnum   **522**

Shepherd of souls, give to us for the leadership of your Church in this parish a man after your own heart:
   a man of faith and prayer, filled with the Spirit;
   a man of vision, wisdom and sound judgment;
   a man with a pastoral heart and a true love for people.
Prepare the man of your choice for his ministry among us, and prepare us for his coming; and overrule in everything for the doing of your will and the furtherance of your glory; through Jesus Christ our Lord.   *Frank Colquhoun*

                                                               523

Lord, call to this your church and ours
      a true shepherd,
      a man of God,
      a minister of Christ;
   and make us, with him,
      a church joyful in worship

and united in witness,
working, caring, praising, loving,
to the glory of your name;
through Jesus Christ our Lord.

Timothy Dudley-Smith

Parish visitors 524

Heavenly Father, you have committed to our care those who
live in this parish. We cannot know all the different people
around us, but we ask that your Holy Spirit will guide us this
week to those situations where we can minister something of
your love and compassion. Help us to rejoice with those who
rejoice, weep with those who weep, and bring practical solutions
to problems we encounter, for Jesus Christ's sake.

Michael Botting

A parish mission 525

Eternal God, lover of the souls of men, you have called us to be
Christ's witnesses in the world and have put us in trust with the
gospel: hear us as we ask your blessing on the mission to be held
in our parish.

May the Holy Spirit guide and empower us and all who share
in this task, so that many may be brought to a knowledge of your
love and may dedicate their lives to your service.

We ask it for the glory of our Lord and Saviour Jesus Christ.

526

Almighty God, our heavenly Father, we ask you to bless
the visit of . . . to this parish.
Go before us in all our preparations,
calling out faithful helpers
and supplying all our needs.

Help us to make sense of the gospel,
   and to relate it to the needs of others,
so that many may be drawn to the Saviour's love
   to worship and serve you in the family of your Church;
through Jesus Christ our Lord.   *Cambridge Pastorate*

527

God of grace and mercy,
   open the eyes of the blind,
   breathe life into the dead,
   release those bound by sin and Satan;
and through your Holy Spirit's power
   may hearts be challenged,
   minds convinced,
   and wills conquered;
in the name of Jesus Christ our Lord.

Michael Saward

528

O God of love, we ask your blessing on the mission to be held
in this parish; that the gospel may be so presented in the power of
the Holy Spirit that both young and old may respond to the claims
of Christ and find newness of life in him, to the praise and glory
of his name.

For a church porch   **529**

No man entering a house ignores him who dwells there.
This is the house of God and he is here.
Pray then to him who loves you and bids you welcome.
Give thanks for those who in years past built this place to his
glory.
Rejoice in his gifts of beauty in art and music, architecture and
handicraft; and worship him, the one God and Father of us all,
through our Lord and Saviour Jesus Christ.   *Adapted*

O God, make the door of this house wide enough
to receive all who need human love and fellowship;
narrow enough to shut out all envy, pride, and strife.
Make its threshold smooth enough to be no stumbling-block to
children,
nor to straying feet, but rugged and strong
to turn back the tempter's power.
God, make the doorway of this house
the entrance to your eternal kingdom.

A DEDICATION FESTIVAL

Thanksgiving and prayer **531**

W<small>E</small> praise you, O Lord, at this time for the remembrance of your goodness to us as a parish: for all who have served this church of . . . through the years that are past, and for its continuing worship and witness in our own day.

Accept our thanksgiving for what you have done; take our lives as we now dedicate them anew to your service; and prosper our endeavours to further Christ's gospel and kingdom in the days to come, for the glory of his name. *Frank Colquhoun*

532

O Holy Spirit of the living God, proceeding from the Father and the Son, Spirit of truth and love, the Lord and the Life-giver, sanctify with your presence this place of prayer.

Here may the people be drawn into your fellowship and conquered by your love; here may the ignorant learn the way of truth, the sinful find pardon, and the weary rest; here may the members of your holy Church be strengthened in the bond of peace and righteousness of life, manfully to confess the faith of Christ crucified.

Fulfil the prayers of those who worship here, hallow their praises and enrich their lives; unite them in the service of the kingdom which has no end, that in all things and by all men your name may be adored, who with the Father and the Son lives and reigns, one God, world without end.

*A Diocesan Service Book**

533

God of all grace, as once again we celebrate the dedication of this church, we praise your holy name for all who have faithfully worshipped and served you here through the years that are past, and especially those whom we would now remember in your presence . . .

May the recollection of their lives and their work kindle in our hearts a sense of gratitude and a strong resolve to preserve and pass on to others what we ourselves have so richly enjoyed; for the honour of our Lord and Saviour Jesus Christ.

A parish church   534

Lord Jesus Christ, whose promise is that wherever two or three are gathered together in your name, you are there in the midst of them: glorify and lighten with your presence this earthly house built to your honour and dedicated to your service; and be pleased both to inspire and accept its worship, the praise of thankful lips and the prayers of faithful hearts, to the glory of your great and glorious name, now and always.   *Adapted*

The priesthood of the Church   535

Eternal and most merciful Father, we praise you for calling your Church out of the darkness of sin into Christ's marvellous light and exalting us to sit with him as kings and priests.

Grant that our worship may be acceptable, our living holy, and our witness effective.

This we ask in the name of our great High Priest, Jesus Christ.
Michael Botting

Dedication to service   536

Lord Jesus Christ, who said to your disciples "Follow me", help us to respond to your call:
to commit ourselves to you as our Saviour and King,
to give our lives to your obedience,

and to serve you faithfully all our days, in the fellowship of
your Church,
for the glory of your holy name.   *Frank Colquhoun*

537

O God our heavenly Father,
    whose Son our Lord Jesus Christ
took the form of a servant
    and became the Man for others:
grant us the same spirit of service
    and help us to follow in his steps,
that with love and humility
    we may give ourselves to those who need our help.
In his name we ask it.   *Frank Colquhoun*

538

O God, our Redeemer and our King, we thankfully acknowledge that to you and to your grace we owe all we are and all we
have.
    We now offer ourselves to you for whatever of life remains to us.
While time is ours,
while health is ours,
while reason is ours,
while opportunity is ours,
    take us, O Lord, and use us as you will in the service of others
and for the furtherance of your kingdom, that in all things your
name may be glorified; through Jesus Christ our Lord.

                                       Frank Colquhoun

539

Almighty God our heavenly Father, whose Son taught us that
every service done for others' sake is done for him: give us the
wisdom, the will, and the strength to be living examples of this
truth, that in serving one another we may glorify him, our Saviour
and our Lord.   *Basil Naylor*

540

God our Father, we offer you our lives
   to do your work in the world.
Help us by your Holy Spirit
   to hear more clearly your call
   to deeper devotedness in your service,
and give us grace to respond with gladness;
   for the glory of Christ our Lord.   *USPG*

541

Lord Jesus, you gave yourself for me upon the cross.
I now give myself to you:
   all that I have,
   all that I am,
   all that I hope to be.
Give me in return your forgiveness,
your love, your courage,
and send me forth in your name and in your service.
                              Alan Warren

542

Heavenly Father, you have appointed for your servants a war
to wage and a kingdom to win: accept and fit us for your service
   Enter, cleanse and inspire our hearts.
   Give to us the spirit not of fear but of power, of love, and of
discipline.
   Lead us to the battle-fields which you have prepared for us
and meet us there with the comfort of your love; that though of
ourselves we can do nothing, yet in your strength and in the
fellowship of your service we may minister to the needs of our
generation and to the coming of your kingdom of peace; through
Jesus Christ our Lord.

CLERGY AND CHURCH WORKERS

Pastors of Christ's flock 543

LORD Jesus Christ, the good Shepherd who laid down your life for the sheep, we pray for those whom you have called to be under-shepherds of your flock [*especially . . .*].

Give them the grace they need to fulfil your charge; pour into their hearts a true love for the people committed to their care; and so guide and govern them by the Holy Spirit that all they do may be for the welfare of your Church, the extension of your kingdom, and to the praise and glory of your name. *Adapted*

544

We thank you, O God, for making man in such a way
   that what he is can respond to what you are:
bless all those whose response to your call
   takes the form of service in the sacred ministry.
Make perfect their desire to be your servants,
   and increase their understanding of man's need
   and your great love.
So may they find power, peace and gladness
   and share the same with those they serve;
through Jesus Christ our Lord. *Dick Williams*

545

Great Shepherd, you have committed your flock to those who serve you as pastors and teachers; give them the ability to lead gently, to teach wisely, and to bring their people to maturity of spirit and holiness of life; in Jesus' name. *Michael Saward*

A parish priest   546

Almighty Father, lover of mankind
  and giver of all that is good:
hear our prayers for your servant
  whom you have called to the charge of this parish.
Strengthen him, O Lord, by your Holy Spirit
  and fill him with love for your people;
that as a faithful priest and true servant of your Son
  he may preach your word,
    minister your sacraments,
    and shepherd your flock,
to the glory of your name;
  through Jesus Christ our Lord.

See also 252–6

Church workers   547

Give us, dear Lord, the modesty to know that the work in
which we are engaged is but a part of the obedience of your whole
Church.

Give us faithfulness to fulfil that part by being all that we are
meant to be and doing only what we are meant to do.

And give us the enthusiasm to share the task with those whom
you have called to serve in other ways, that together we may
proclaim your great salvation; through Jesus Christ our Lord.

Church Missionary Society

548

Almighty God, you have given us a neighbourhood to serve
and a gospel to proclaim.

Renew us with your Spirit, that in worship and in service we
may be true to our profession as fellow-workers with Christ in
his mission to the world, for the glory of his name.

Basil Naylor

549

Living Lord, we thank you for the honour and joy of being called to your service in the fellowship of your Church.

Help us never to grow weary in well-doing;

make us always ready to give a reason for the hope that is in us;

and keep us faithful and vigilant as servants who wait for their Lord.

We ask it for your name's sake. *Michael Botting*

550

Lord, make us more effective witnesses for the gospel and deepen our understanding of the faith; that our convictions may be so strong that we shall want to share them, and so lucid that we shall know how to communicate them; for the honour of our Lord Jesus Christ.

Based on words of Bishop Mervyn Stockwood

551

Lord, in all our work for you teach us how to rest as well as how to labour; how to listen as well as how to speak; how to receive service as well as how to render it; and save us both from foolish pride and from false modesty; through Jesus Christ our Lord. *Response*

552

Almighty God, by whose grace alone we have been accepted and called to your service: strengthen and guide us by your Holy Spirit in all our work and make us worthy of our calling; through Jesus Christ our Lord. *A Christian's Prayer Book*

553

Lord Jesus, Saviour of mankind, give us such an understanding of your love that we may have courage to witness for you boldly, compassion for people in need, and readiness to obey your call to make disciples of all nations, for the glory of your name.

A prayer for renewal   **554**

Renew us, O Lord our God:
  renew our faith in your purpose for mankind;
  renew our obedience to your commands;
  renew our commitment to the mission of your Church;
  renew our love, our hope and our joy
in your Son Jesus Christ our Lord.

Church Missionary Society★

CHURCH MEETINGS

Parochial church council

LORD Christ, Son of God, you have promised that where two or three meet together in your name, there you are in the midst of them. We claim that promise now for ourselves as we come together to do your work and to take counsel one with another; and we pray that in the light of your presence we may face the tasks before us, consider our problems, make our decisions, and so exercise a faithful stewardship, for the good of your Church and for the glory of your name.   *Frank Colquhoun*

556

O God our heavenly Father, in whose name we are now met together in the service of your kingdom: we pray that the Holy Spirit may guide our minds and order our wills as we take counsel one with another; so that all our concerns and endeavours may be directed to the strengthening of your work in this parish, and to the furtherance of the Church's mission in the world; through Jesus Christ our Lord.   *Frank Colquhoun*

557

O Holy Spirit of God, we ask for your presence and guidance at the meeting of the church council [*this week*].

May each member of the council exercise his or her responsibilities wisely and prayerfully, and may the decisions of the council be in accordance with your will and for the extension of Christ's kingdom in this parish, for his name's sake.

Peter Markby

The annual church meeting 558

Almighty God, we come together this evening in the service of your Church to remember with thanksgiving all that you have been able to do through us in this parish during the past year, and to seek your guidance in the elections for the coming year.

We pray that this may be something more than just a business meeting but rather an occasion when we receive fresh encouragement in our work, catch a wider vision of your purpose, and dedicate ourselves anew to your service.

We ask this in the name of him who came to this world not to be served but to serve, and gave his life as a ransom for many, Jesus Christ our Lord. *Michael Botting*

Before a committee meeting 559

Lord God, you have taught us in your word that we are members of the one body of Christ, each with a place to fill and a function to perform: in this task which you have given us to do together enable us by your grace to make our varying contributions humbly and unselfishly, to work in love and harmony one with another, and to serve to your honour and not our own, in the name of Christ our Lord.

*Presbyterian Church of England**

560

Heavenly Father, giver of all good gifts, hear us as we seek the blessing of the Holy Spirit on what we say and do in this meeting.

We acknowledge our shortcomings and limitations, our ignorance, our pride, our lack of faith.

Forgive us, O Lord; cleanse us, illuminate us, direct us, use us; and grant that nothing in our lives may hinder your work, but that in all things we may set forward the cause of Christ and his kingdom, for the glory of his name. *Frank Colquhoun*

561

Guide and undertake, O Lord,
   in all that lies before us in this meeting.
May the Holy Spirit direct us
   in our thinking and our speaking,
     and give us understanding of your will;
for the furtherance of Christ's kingdom
     and the glory of your name.   *Frank Colquhoun*

562

Holy Spirit of God, source of knowledge
   and creator of fellowship:
open our minds to recognize the truth
   and our hearts to welcome it,
that in company together we may learn your will
   and be strengthened to obey it;
through Jesus Christ our Lord.   *Basil Naylor*

563

Lord, guide us as we meet together, that we may think calmly
and carefully, decide wisely and well, in order that everything
may be done in accordance with your will. Help us to make your
concerns our concerns, so that through us you may be able to
carry on your work here on earth; for Jesus Christ's sake.
   John D. Searle

After a meeting   **564**

We thank you, O God, for your presence among us in this
meeting, guiding our thoughts and strengthening our fellowship
one with another in your service.

Whatever we have now agreed to do, in accordance with your
will, give us the grace and power to fulfil, to the glory of your
name; and may your blessing continually rest upon us in all our
work together; through Jesus Christ our Lord.   *Adapted*

A finance committee 565

Heavenly Father, this is your work in which we are engaged, for the world is yours and all that is in it, and we are stewards, not owners, of the things we possess.

Make us mindful of this in our meeting today; and may the Spirit of Christ so direct us in all we say and do that we may exercise our stewardship faithfully and wisely, for the good of your Church and the glory of your name.   *Frank Colquhoun*

A missionary meeting 566

Sanctify our gathering together with your presence, O Lord.
May your Word quicken the words to be spoken;
may your Spirit enlighten the hearts that shall receive them;
and may your love unite us in a community of loving concern;
that the place which this work has in your holy will and purpose may be faithfully mirrored in the life of your Church; through Jesus Christ our Lord.   *Dick Williams*★

PARISH GROUPS

Children of the Church **567**

HEAVENLY Father, you have taught us that all children are embraced by your love and under your care: look in your tender mercy on the children you have entrusted to us.

In their weakness hold them in the arms of your strength, and in their simplicity turn their hearts to the Good Shepherd of all your sheep, your Son Jesus Christ our Lord.

F. G. Kerr-Dineen

568

Father, you have entrusted to our care
    the children of your Church,
and have charged us to guide and train them
    in the way of Christ.
Help us to be faithful to our trust,
    both in our teaching and our prayers;
that our boys and girls may grow up
    in the knowledge of your love,
to worship and serve you all their days
    as members of your family,
        to the honour and glory of your name.

Frank Colquhoun

Teachers **569**

Holy Spirit of truth, enlighten the minds of those who teach the children of the Church and give them the love, patience and

understanding they need for their task; that those committed to
their care may grow in grace and in the knowledge of our Lord
and Saviour Jesus Christ, to the praise and glory of his name.

Frank Colquhoun

A youth group 570

Jesus, Lord and Saviour, we ask your blessing upon those who
are joined together in the youth group of this parish.

Help them so to think and pray and work together that they
may become one in purpose to seek your will for their lives and
to worship and serve you loyally in the fellowship of your Church.

We ask it in your name, Christ our Lord.   *Adapted*

571

Heavenly Father, whose Son Jesus Christ is the same yesterday
and today and for ever, with a word and purpose for every
generation: give those who are meeting here the will to hear and
receive that word, and equip them with the power to carry out
that purpose in their lives, to the glory of your name.

Basil Naylor

Young people 572

Lord of all grace and power, we ask you to send your blessing
on the young people of our church.

May they enjoy to the full the good things you have prepared
for them and learn to use them rightly and unselfishly, thinking
of others as well as of themselves.

Guide their lives according to your will, and strengthen them
for the work to which you are calling them.

We ask it in the name of our Saviour Jesus Christ.   *Adapted*

Youth leaders 573

Heavenly Father, we praise you for providing leaders as gifts to your Church, for building up your people in faith and love.

We pray for the leaders of this youth club; equip them with every needful grace for all the demands made upon them, so that they may serve with humility and love, with perseverance and zeal, and in the name of Jesus Christ our Lord.

Christopher Idle

Young and old 574

Grant, our Father, that in this church
the younger may respect the traditions of the older,
and the older may understand the impatience of the younger;
so that young and old may share together in your service
and gladly recognize that all are one
in Jesus Christ our Lord. *Christopher Idle*

Men's group 575

Strong Son of God, our Saviour, who chose for your first followers not the great or exalted but ordinary men from the common ways of life, and gave them each a place in your service: we thank you for calling us to serve you in the fellowship of the Church in this our day.

Keep us faithful to our calling; strengthen the bonds of brotherhood that unite us to each other; and show us how best we may bear our witness as Christian men in our homes, our places of work, and in the life of our community, to the honour and praise of your name. *Frank Colquhoun*

Women's fellowship 576

Jesus, Word of the Father, born of a woman, who in your days here on earth companied with Mary and Martha in their home at Bethany: we ask your blessing on the homes from which we have come today and to which we shall be returning; and as we now meet together in this hour of fellowship we pray that we may know your presence with us and find strength and refreshment to serve you better in our daily life.

We ask it for your love's sake.   *Frank Colquhoun*

Women of the Church   577

Almighty God, who in the fullness of time
    sent forth your Son, born of a woman:
pour out your grace and heavenly blessing
    on all women of the church.
Grant that as Jesus numbered women among his followers
    and received their ministry in his life
    and at his death,
so the women of our day may serve
    as the handmaids of the Lord,
adorned with the gifts and graces of the Holy Spirit,
    to tell out the greatness of the Lord
    to this and to all generations;
for the sake of Jesus Christ our Lord.   *Llewellyn Cumings*

Before a study group   578

Lord Christ, as we meet together in your name, prepare us in heart and mind to listen to what you have to say to us.

Help us, too, to listen to one another, so that we may help each other to grasp your will for us.

Deepen and enrich our fellowship as members of your body; inspire us with a deep longing for your truth; and enable us to grow together in knowledge, in love, and in the joyous freedom of the sons of God; for your name's sake.

*Presbyterian Church of England**

CHURCH MUSIC

For a church choir **579**

O LORD God, whose glory the heavens are telling
in joyous and ceaseless praise:
accept the service of those
who sing in the choir of this church.
May they worship you with true devotion,
and by their music uplift the hearts of your people
in faith, thanksgiving, and adoration;
through Jesus Christ our Lord.   *Roger Pickering*

580

Bless, O God, those who sing in the choir of this church, that
with heart and voice they may make melody to the Lord; and
may they so lead our praises that together we may magnify your
glorious name, through Jesus Christ our Saviour.

Frank Colquhoun

Before a choir practice **581**

We thank you, O Lord our God, for calling us to your service
in the ministry of praise.
Teach us to serve you faithfully as members of this choir;
help us always to give of our best in our worship;
and may our lives as well as our lips show forth your praise;
for the honour of our Lord and Saviour Jesus Christ.

Frank Colquhoun

Almighty God, we thank you for uniting us in this choir through the singing of your praises.

Help us so to continue in love for you that our lives may daily reflect your glory.

We ask this in the name of Jesus Christ our Lord.

Douglas Caiger

A choir festival 583

Eternal God, source of all beauty and harmony, we praise you for the gift of music:

for the inspiration given to those who compose it,

for the skill and devotion of those who perform it,

for the faculties and powers which enable us to enjoy it;

and we pray that you will sanctify and accept the music to be rendered in this church today, and make it an offering of praise to the glory of your holy name; through Jesus Christ our Lord.

Frank Colquhoun

584

O Lord Jesus Christ, whose birth was heralded by angels' song, and whose death for sinners is extolled by the music of heaven: grant that those who use voices and instruments to show your glory may also display in their lives that harmony which echoes your praise; for your own name's sake. *Christopher Idle*

Before hymn-singing 585

Almighty God, our heavenly Father, you have taught us to offer our praise in psalms and hymns and spiritual songs, to sing and make melody to you with all our hearts: bless to our use the hymns to be sung in this church, that they may bring enrichment to our worship, joy and strength to our lives, and ever greater glory to your name; through Jesus Christ our Lord.

Frank Colquhoun

HOLY COMMUNION

For reflection—1 586

OUR Lord Jesus Christ said:
I am the bread of life. Whoever comes to me shall never be hungry, and whoever believes in me shall never be thirsty.
I am the living bread which has come down from heaven: if anyone eats this bread he shall live for ever. Moreover, the bread which I will give is my own flesh; I give it for the life of the world.
My flesh is real food; my blood is real drink. Whoever eats my flesh and drinks my blood dwells continually in me and I dwell in him.

Here I stand knocking at the door;
    if anyone hears my voice and opens the door,
I will come in and sit down to supper with him,
    and he with me.

St. John 6. 35, 51, 55, 56;
Revelation 3. 20 (NEB)

For reflection—2 587

The apostle Paul wrote:
    The cup of blessing which we bless,
        is it not a participation in the blood of Christ?
    The bread which we break,
        is it not a participation in the body of Christ?
    Because there is one loaf, we who are many are one body,
        for we all partake of the same loaf.

As often as you eat this bread and drink the cup,
    you proclaim the Lord's death until he comes.
Whoever therefore eats the bread or drinks the cup
    of the Lord in an unworthy manner,
    will be guilty of profaning the body and blood of the Lord.
Let a man examine himself,
    and so eat of the bread and drink of the cup.

                1 Corinthians 10. 16, 17; 11. 26–9 (RSV)

For reflection—3   **588**

    Let us reflect how in the Holy Communion
        the night of Christ's birth,
        the night in which he was betrayed,
        the hours upon the cross,
        the morning of resurrection,
        the glory of the ascension,
        and our own worship and need
    are brought together in one eternal moment.

    Let us thank God that throughout the world
        the Holy Communion is the most loved
        and solemn act of Christian worship;
    that in this sacrament Christ comes to us
        in forgiveness and love,
        to unite us to himself,
        to transform us for his service.   *George Appleton*

Thanksgiving   **589**

    O God, our Father, we thank you for this sacrament;
    for all who down the centuries at your table have found
        the light that never fades;
        the joy that no man takes from them;

the forgiveness of their sins;
the love which is your love;
the presence of their Lord;
    we thank you.   *Worship Now*

Preparation for communion   **590**

Come to us, Lord Christ, in your risen glory, and preside as host at your table in the sacrament of your body and blood.

May it be to us not only a memorial of your saving passion but a means of grace to our souls, a pledge of our eternal inheritance, and a sign of our unity within the body of your Church;

that renewed in spirit we may live more truly as your disciples and show your glory before the world; for the honour of your holy name.   *Frank Colquhoun*

591

Merciful God, we do not dare to come to your table
    trusting in our own goodness and virtue.
We come because we are sinful men
    and need forgiveness.
We come because we are hungry for life
    and need to be fed.
Father, forgive and feed us.
We come because Christ has invited us sinners.
We come in gratitude and wonder
    to offer our very selves to you
    in worship and adoration.
Father, accept our praise,
    through Jesus Christ our Lord.
            Contemporary Prayers for Public Worship

592

Most gracious God, we look forward to the holy communion tomorrow.

We desire to enter into the presence of your most holy Son, and there to remain;

to join with your whole Church in offering the holy sacrifice, that you may be worshipped and glorified;

to receive the life of your Son and to be stamped with his character;

to offer to you ourselves, and to be attentive and recollected;

that your purpose of love may be fulfilled to the honour and glory of your name; through Jesus Christ our Lord.

R. Somerset Ward

593

Lord, the feast is yours,
    not ours.
It is your table to which we come,
    to be your guests.
It is your presence we seek,
    your body and blood of which we partake.
Help us to draw near with expectant hearts
    and a living faith,
to receive as from your hands
    the bread of life,
    the cup of salvation,
and so to find refreshment, strength and peace;
    for your love's sake.   *Frank Colquhoun*

594

Our gracious Lord, we recall how on that solemn passover night before you suffered for our redemption you gave your disciples the bread and the wine to be your body and blood, and said to them "Do this in remembrance of me".

As we prepare to obey your word and to gather at your table
[in the morning] we pray that we may have a deepened understanding of your love and all that you have done for us; so that
we may come with joyful and expectant hearts to offer you the
sacrifice of our praise and thanksgiving and to meet with you,
our risen Lord; to whom be glory, honour and might for ever
and ever. *Frank Colquhoun*

595

Give us the grace, our Father, to judge ourselves before we are
judged by you;
    to repent truly of past sin;
    to have a lively and steady faith in Christ our Saviour;
    and to be willing to live more faithfully to you from now on.
You sent your Son to give himself for us; may we prove our
love by giving ourselves to you, and serving you for his sake
every day of our life. *Christopher Idle*

596

Come Lord Jesus, in the fullness of your grace,
    and dwell in the hearts of us your servants;
    that adoring you by faith
        we may with joy receive you,
    and may with love and thankfulness abide in you,
        our Guide, our Bread of pilgrims,
        our Comrade by the way. *E. D. Sedding, SSJE*

After communion   **597**

Strengthen for service, O Lord,
    the hands that have taken holy things.
May the ears that have heard your word
    be deaf to clamour and dispute;
    may the tongues that have sung your praise
    be free from deceit;

may the eyes that have seen the tokens of your love
shine with the light of hope;
and may the bodies which have been fed with your Body
be replenished with the fullness of your life.

Based on the Liturgy of Malabar

598

Father, we thank you that once more you have fed us with the Bread of Life.

We thank you for our fellowship with you, and with each other, and with all the people of God, on earth and in heaven, especially those most dear to us, whom now for a little while we see no more.

We thank you that nothing can separate us from your love in Christ, to whom with you and the Holy Spirit be glory and dominion throughout all ages.   *Worship Now*

599

Gracious God, we say a blessing for a Father's gifts, and we go away to live by them, at home and at work.

Grant us to see in every family table an image of the communion table;

to see in all the daily bread shared at home the sign of your providing and protecting;

and to carry into all our converse, at home and with friends, something of the fellowship of the Church.

And unite us in the Spirit here and everywhere with the rest of your family, divided from us by distance, or by death, until the day of our last homecoming to you; through Jesus Christ our Lord.   *Worship Now*

See also 91–2

BAPTISM AND CONFIRMATION

Thanksgiving 600

HEAVENLY Father, we thank you that in uniting us with Christ in our baptism you have made us one with all members of your worldwide Church. You have also made us new creatures: the old life is over, the new life has begun.

Accept our praise for this; and help us to glorify you by daily dying to sin and rising to righteousness, in fellowship with all Christ's people everywhere, for his name's sake.   *Adapted*

The life of the baptized 601

Help us, O Lord our God, always to remember
    that when we were baptized into union with Christ
we were baptized into his death,
    that we might be crucified with him and die to sin.
And we pray that as Christ was raised from the dead
    by your glorious power,
so we may now walk in newness of life
    as those who are no longer under the dominion
    of sin and death;
through the same Jesus Christ our Lord.

Based on Romans 6. 1–11

The new covenant 602

O God, who through the passion of your Son made a new covenant of grace with mankind: grant that we who by baptism and faith have entered into that covenant may continue in faith, rejoice in hope, and abound in love, as servants of our Lord and Saviour Jesus Christ.

Those bringing their children to baptism 603

O God our Father, from whom every family in heaven and earth takes its name: be present to bless the families of the children soon to be baptized as members of your Church.

Help the parents and godparents to see the meaning of your saving gospel; to make their promises sincerely and heartily; to pray for their children; and to teach them of holy things; so that they may all share in your gift of eternal life; in the name of Jesus Christ our Lord. *Christopher Idle*

Children baptized 604

Heavenly Father and giver of all grace, we ask your blessing on those who in baptism have received the seal of the new covenant and been made heirs of your heavenly kingdom; that through the prayers, the teaching, and the example of those who love and care for them they may grow up in the faith of Christ crucified and in the fellowship of his Church, to serve you faithfully all the days of their life; through Jesus Christ our Lord.

Frank Colquhoun

605

Lord Jesus Christ, because you welcomed the little ones who were brought to you, we pray for those who this morning [*or* afternoon, evening] were added to the fellowship of your Church.

Guard them in health and strength as they grow up; help their parents to trust you and to make their homes your dwelling; and use the children's work of this church to nourish their faith in you; for the glory of your saving name. *Christopher Idle*

Homes and parents **606**

God our Father, whose Son our Lord grew up in a home at Nazareth: we pray for the home of this child, that it may be hallowed by prayer and be the abode of love, joy and peace.

Give to *his* parents care and understanding in the training of their child; and may they by their teaching and example lead *him* in the way of Christ, that *he* may grow in grace and in the knowledge of your love; for the honour and glory of your name.

Adapted

607

Give understanding and strength, O God our Father, to the parents of this child, that they may daily keep their promise to bring *him* up in the faith of Christ and in the fellowship of his Church.

Shed your blessing upon them in their home, and may the spirit of love and peace abide with them always.

We ask it in Christ's name. *Frank Colquhoun*

See also the baptism of Jesus, 57–8

CONFIRMATION

Those preparing for confirmation **608**

HEAVENLY Father, we bring to you in our prayers those who at this time are preparing for confirmation. So work in their hearts by your Holy Spirit that they may be ready to receive all that you are seeking to teach them, and to dedicate their lives to your service; and by your grace keep them faithful to their promises all the days of their life; through Jesus Christ our Lord.

Frank Colquhoun

609

Hear our prayer, O God, for those who are shortly to be confirmed.

Let this be, for each of them, no formal step.

Give them a living faith in your Son Jesus Christ as their Redeemer and King, and grace to confess him before men; that filled with his Spirit, and strengthened by the Bread of life, they may serve you faithfully all their days; through the same Jesus Christ our Lord. *Frank Colquhoun*

610

God our Father, you choose and call and equip men and women for the work of your kingdom: give to those who will soon be confirmed a mature faith, a confident hope, and a sincere love, by the ministry of your Holy Spirit; that your Church may be enriched by their fellowship and they may be effective in your service; through Jesus Christ our Lord. *Christopher Idle*

611

O Lord and heavenly Father,
you are calling us to give you a lifetime of service
and to receive your strength through confirmation.
Open our hearts to receive all that you want to give,
so that in lives made strong by your Holy Spirit
we may serve you gladly and bravely all our days,
in the name of Jesus Christ our Lord. *Roger Pickering*

612

Heavenly Father, we pray for each of our friends here who are soon to be confirmed. Keep them firm and faithful in the promises which they will make; and as we welcome them into the full membership of the Church, so let them be filled with the power, the love and the joy of your Spirit; through Jesus Christ our Lord.
Alan Warren

Before a confirmation class **613**

Lord Jesus Christ, we read of how on various occasions you took your disciples apart by themselves and taught them many things.

As we prepare for our confirmation we come to you now for instruction.

Show us, O Lord, what it means to be a Christian in the world of today.

Teach us more about yourself, more about our faith, more about the life of discipleship; and help us to love you more because of your great love for us.

We ask this for your name's sake. *Frank Colquhoun*

The newly confirmed **614**

We thank you, our God and Father, for those who in confirmation have made confession of their faith and have been welcomed into the communicant life of the Christian family in this place.

Help us each one, by our prayers, our friendship and our example, to encourage them in the way of Christ, that they may fully grow up into him and continue steadfastly in the worship and fellowship of the Church, to the glory of your name; through Jesus Christ our Lord. *Frank Colquhoun*

MARRIAGE

At the publication of banns **615**

SEND your blessing, heavenly Father, upon these your servants;
that making Christ the sure foundation of their earthly home,
they may live together in holy love until their lives' end, and after
this life dwell with you for ever in heaven; through Jesus Christ
our Lord. *F. G. Kerr-Dineen*

616

Heavenly Father, bless these your servants N. and N., that the
marriage for which they now prepare themselves may be built
upon the strong foundation of their love for you as well as for
each other, and the home which they shall build may ever know
your presence, your joy, and your peace. *Gordon Hyslop*

617

O Lord our God, giver of all good things, we ask your blessing
upon these your servants whose lives are shortly to be joined in
marriage. May they dwell together in love and peace all the days
of their life, seeking one another's welfare, bearing one another's
burdens, and sharing one another's joys; through Jesus Christ our
Lord. *Adapted*

Those preparing for marriage **618**

Most merciful God, by whom the solitary are set in families,
we pray that your blessing may rest upon N. and N. as they
prepare for their wedding.

May their marriage be for them a source of great and lasting good. Spare them long to each other, and keep them faithful, tender, and true, so that they may live together in peace and happiness; and may your blessing be upon them in their home and in all the work of their hands; for the sake of Jesus Christ our Lord. *Worship Now**

Dedication of a ring 619

In your name, O Lord, we dedicate this ring;
and we pray that he who gives it
and she who wears it
may keep true faith one with another,
and remain in unbroken love to their lives' end.

Adapted

Marriage, the basis of society 620

Eternal God, author of harmony and happiness, we thank you for the gift of marriage in which men and women seek and find fulfilment, companionship, and the blessing of family life.

Give patience to those who look forward to marriage.
Give courage to those who face trials within their marriage.
Give comfort to those whose marriage has broken.
Give gratitude to those whose marriages are successful and fruitful, and let their lives reflect your love and your glory.
Through Jesus Christ our Lord. *Michael Saward**

Marriage Guidance counsellors 621

O God our Father, whose Son our Lord blessed the marriage at Cana in Galilee by his presence and the first of his miracles; hear our prayer for all who seek to counsel those whose marriages are at risk.

Give them sympathy, understanding, and insight into the needs of others; and so use them in this service that by your grace hurts may be healed, faults forgiven, and misunderstandings removed. We ask this prayer in the name of Jesus Christ our Saviour.

Llewellyn Cumings

For the blessing of a civil marriage   **622**

Almighty God, Lord of all life and giver of all joy, we pray for these your servants, *N.* and *N.*, who desire to offer their lives to you in holy matrimony. Grant that in simple trust they may commit themselves to your keeping and be given grace to live together in mutual love and fidelity, to the honour of your name; through Jesus Christ our Lord.

623

O God of love, look mercifully upon your servants *N.* and *N.* who seek your help and guidance for the new life which they begin together this day.

Unite them evermore in your love.

Keep them faithful to the vows they have made one to the other.

Enrich them in their married life with every good gift.

And let your peace be with them, now and always; for the sake of Jesus Christ our Lord.

The above two prayers are adapted from prayers used in various dioceses

624

Heavenly Father, giver of all good things, may your blessing rest upon the home which your servants will build together. Sanctify it with your presence, and make it to abound in peace and love; through Jesus Christ our Lord.   *Frank Colquhoun*

FUNERALS AND
MEMORIAL SERVICES

Thanksgiving   625

A LMIGHTY God, from whose love
    neither death nor life can separate us:
with the whole company of the redeemed,
    in heaven and on earth,
we praise and magnify your glorious name,
    Father, Son, and Holy Spirit,
    one God, blessed for ever.

                                                                626

Blessed be the God and Father
    of our Lord Jesus Christ!
By his great mercy we have been born anew
    to a living hope
through the resurrection of Jesus Christ
    from the dead,
and to an inheritance which is imperishable,
    undefiled and unfading,
reserved in heaven
    for all who put their faith in God.

Based on 1 Peter 1. 3–5

The Christian hope   627

We praise you, O God our Father, for the hope of our calling:
for the victory of our Lord Jesus Christ, who has broken the
power of death and brought life and immortality to light through
the gospel;

for the eternal home which he has gone to prepare for us, and
for his promise to come again and receive us to himself;

for the great multitude which no man can number, out of every
nation, who stand before the throne, and with whom in our Lord
we for evermore are one. *Frank Colquhoun*

628

We thank you, O Lord our God,
 that the life which we now live in Christ
 is part of the life which is eternal,
and the fellowship which we have in him
 unites us with your whole Church
 on earth and in heaven;
and we pray that as we journey through the years
 we may know joys which are without end,
and at last come to that abiding city
 where you reign for evermore. *New Every Morning*

Commemoration of the departed   629

Almighty God, Father of all mercies, we offer you our praise
for all who have lived and died in the faith of your holy name, and
especially for *him* whom we now remember before you with love
and thanksgiving.

Give us grace to be faithful in the days of our earthly pilgrim-
age, that with them we may share the glory of your heavenly
kingdom and be partakers of their joy; through the merits of our
Saviour Jesus Christ, to whom with you and the Holy Spirit be
praise and glory for ever and ever.

630

Eternal God and Father,
 whose love is stronger than death,
we rejoice that the dead as well as the living
 are in your love and care;

and as we remember with thanksgiving
   those who have gone before us
   in the way of Christ,
we pray that we may be counted worthy
   to share with them the life of your kingdom;
through Jesus Christ our Lord.   *James M. Todd*

631

We thank you, our Father, that our loved ones who have gone from our sight are in your keeping.

Help us to leave them there in perfect trust, because you love them and us with infinite love.

Grant that we may learn to know you better, so that we may meet them again in your presence, through faith in him who loved us and gave himself for us, Jesus Christ our Saviour.

       R. E. Cleeve

632

Most merciful God, who in your loving kindness gave us so much joy through your servants departed: we thank you for them and for our memories of them.

We praise you for your goodness and mercy that followed them all the days of their life, and for their faithfulness in the tasks to which you called them.

We bless you that for them the tribulations of this world are over, and death is past; and we pray that you will bring us with them to the joy of your perfect kingdom; through Jesus Christ our Lord.

633

Lord God, Creator of all men, you have made us creatures of this earth, but have also promised us a share in eternal life. May all who have died share this eternal life with your saints in heaven, where there is neither sorrow nor pain, but life everlasting. We ask you this through Christ our Lord.

       A Christian's Prayer Book

634

We thank you, Lord God,
for the grace you gave
to those who lived according to your will
and are now at rest.
We pray that their good example
may encourage and guide us
all the days of our life;
through Jesus Christ our Lord.

The Church in Wales

Those who mourn

635

Jesus, Lord of life and conqueror of death, who dried the tears of the widow at Nain; look with compassion on those who grieve for the loss of one dear to them. Make them to know that you are with them even in the darkest hours, and in your presence may they find courage, comfort and peace; for your love's sake.

Frank Colquhoun

636

Lord Christ, you spoke words of comfort to your friends Martha and Mary in their hour of sorrow. Give consolation and courage to those who mourn today, and may they find their peace and hope in you, the Resurrection and the Life; for your tender mercies' sake.

Adapted

637

Heavenly Father, our refuge and strength in every time of need: help and comfort us today. Increase our faith, dispel our fears, revive our hope; and lift us from the darkness of our grief to the light of your presence; through Jesus Christ our Lord.

*The Church in Wales**

638

O Lord Jesus Christ, who wept at the grave of Lazarus, we commend to your tender care and compassion those whose loss is greatest at this time, because their lives were closest and their love was strongest.

In the midst of their deep sorrow give them the comfort of your presence, and the courage and faith they need to face life again in the days to come. And may your peace be with them, O Lord, both now and always.

See also 421–4

A prayer for suicides **639**

Almighty God, Father of all mankind, have mercy on all those who in their darkness have thrown away their mortal lives. Grant them light and salvation, that they may find new life in your love and glorify your holy name. *Audrey Marshall*

Burial of ashes after cremation **640**

Believing that our *brother* is at rest in Christ, and rejoicing in the communion of saints, we commit *his* ashes to the ground, in sure and certain hope of the resurrection to eternal life; through Jesus Christ our Lord.

Concluding prayer **641**

Grant, O Lord, that we may walk in your presence, with your love in our hearts, your truth in our minds, your strength in our wills; that when we finally stand before you, it may be with the assurance of your welcome and the joy of our homecoming.

George Appleton

VESTRY AND PULPIT PRAYERS

Before service 642

ETERNAL God, help us to remember your presence with us now as we lead the worship of your people; and may their hearts and ours be lifted up in humble prayer and joyful praise, to the glory of our Lord Jesus Christ.

643

Prepare us, O God, for the worship of your house, and give us grace to serve you with reverence, joy, and thanksgiving; through Jesus Christ our Lord.

644

Father, as we now prepare to share in the activity of worship, cleanse our hearts and minds, fill us with your Holy Spirit, and open our lips to show forth your praise; for the sake of Jesus Christ our Lord.

645

O Lord, open our lips and tune our hearts to sing your praise; and make us now and always more worthy of your service; for Jesus Christ's sake.

646

Enable us, O God, to lift up our hearts with our voices as we sing your praise, that in all things we may glorify your holy name, through Jesus Christ our Lord.

Before holy communion **647**

Lord Jesus, stand among us now in your risen power, and make yourself known to us in the breaking of the bread, to the praise and glory of your name.

After service **648**

Accept, O God, the worship of our hearts and of our lips, and give us grace to glorify you in our lives, for the sake of Jesus Christ our Lord.

649

Father, forgive all that has been unworthy in our worship; accept the praise we have offered; and bless to us the words we have heard and sung this day; through Jesus Christ our Lord.

650

Accept, O Lord, the songs of praise we have offered now in church, and help us to carry the spirit of praise into our daily life, for the glory of your holy name.

651

Accept, O God, this our sacrifice of praise; and grant that our worship here on earth may reflect the beauty and harmony of heaven and prepare us for our worship there; through Jesus Christ our Lord.

After holy communion **652**

Grant, our Father, that we who have worshipped at your table may serve you as those who are redeemed by the blood of Christ; and strengthen us always with the Bread of Life, through the same Jesus Christ our Lord. *F. G. Kerr-Dineen*

653

Graciously accept, O God, this our eucharist, the sacrifice of our praise and thanksgiving, and fill our hearts with the joy of your salvation, now and always.

654

Worthy is the Lamb who was slain to receive power and riches, and wisdom and strength, and honour and glory and blessing.

Revelation 5. 12

Before the sermon　　　　　　　　　　　　　　　**655**

O God, open your Word to our hearts, and our hearts to your Word, and give us grace to receive it, to understand it, and to obey it, for the glory of Christ our Lord.

656

Help us, O God, to hear your Word with attention and understanding; and so write its message on our hearts that its power may be manifest in our lives, for the glory of our Lord Jesus Christ.

657

Enable us, our Father, to respond to the grace of your word with humility of heart and in the spirit of love; that our lives may be conformed more and more to the image of your Son, Jesus Christ our Lord.

658

O God, help us to listen to your Word with understanding, to receive it with faith, and to obey it with courage, for Jesus Christ's sake.

659

May the Lord now be in all our hearts, and upon my lips, that every thought and word may be wholly for the honour and glory of his name.

660

Grant, O God, that in the written word, and through the spoken word, we may behold the living Word, our Lord and Saviour Jesus Christ.

VARIOUS

In the morning

HEAVENLY Father, whose mercies are new every morning,
  lead us all through this day,
and help us to follow step by step with trustful hearts,
  steadfast and unafraid.
Make us equal to all that the day may demand of us;
  save us from wasting its hours;
and bring us to its end with something accomplished
  for your glory and your praise.   *Response*

662

Into the hands of your love and mercy, O God our Father, we
commit our lives this day:
  our work and the tasks that await us;
  our homes and the members of our families;
  our loved ones, and especially those in need.
  Give to us your guidance, your strength, and your protection,
according to our needs, and throughout this day keep us abiding
in your love; through Jesus Christ our Lord. *Frank Colquhoun*

Sunday morning

O Lord, our Creator and Redeemer, as you have given us this
day for worship, so now we bring to you the service of our hearts
and hands and voices.
  Accept our prayers and praises; speak to us through the Bible
as we hear it read and taught; deepen our fellowship one with
another; and when we leave your house may it be with your joy
in our hearts; through Jesus Christ our Lord.

A family prayer in the morning   **664**

    For morning light and the gift of a new day,
        we praise you, our heavenly Father;
    and with thankful hearts we now entrust ourselves
        and those we love into your hands,
    praying that you will help us,
        guide us, and keep us
    in all that lies before us this day;
        for the sake of Jesus Christ our Lord.

                                     Frank Colquhoun

A family prayer at evening   **665**

    O God of all life,
        thank you for looking after us today
        and for all your goodness to us.
    Bless us tonight with your forgiveness,
        send your peace into our hearts,
    and take us and all we love into your care;
        for Jesus Christ our Saviour's sake.

An evening intercession   **666**

    Our Father, we are mindful as we come to you in this evening
hour not only of our own needs but also of the needs of others.
    Relieve and heal the sick;
    console the sorrowing and the lonely;
    guide the anxious and perplexed;
    have in your keeping those who face danger this night;
    and be near to all whom we love;
for the sake of Jesus Christ our Lord.   *Frank Colquhoun*

Saturday evening **667**

Almighty and everliving God, before whose presence the angels bow in ceaseless adoration, receive our prayers for the worship to be offered in this church tomorrow.

Give your grace to all who shall speak or read or sing or serve, all who shall kneel at your altar, and all who come to listen and to pray; and grant your blessing to the other parishes in this deanery and diocese, that with one heart and mind we may offer the sacrifice of our praise and thanksgiving, to the glory of your name; through Jesus Christ our Lord. *Sydney Linton*

Stewardship **668**

God our Father, make us to think more of what we can give to life and less of what we can get out of it.

May we be mindful that we hold our gifts, our talents, our possessions, our life itself, in trust for you and the service of mankind.

Save us from thinking only of our own needs and desires; and help us to remember that it is more blessed to give than to receive, according to the teaching of our Lord and Saviour Jesus Christ.

Adapted

669

From greed and avarice, from selfishness in getting and spending, from meanness and miserliness, deliver us, good Lord; and when we are entrusted with gifts of money, help us to spend wisely, to give generously, and to think of the needs of others. This we ask for Christ's sake. *Prayers at School**

670

Jesus, Lord and Master, teach us and all your people so to follow the pattern of your manhood that we may learn to interpret life in terms of giving, not of getting; to be faithful stewards of our time and talents and all that you have entrusted to us; and to buy up every opportunity of serving the needs of others and advancing your kingdom in the world, for the glory of your name. *Frank Colquhoun*

Offertory prayers **671**

We thank you, O Lord, for all your gifts,
    which we receive as tokens of your love to us.
Accept these gifts which we now bring to you
    as tokens of our gratitude,
and use both them and us in the service of your kingdom,
    for Jesus Christ's sake. *Frank Colquhoun*

672

We praise you, Lord Jesus Christ,
    for your generosity:
you were rich, yet for our sake
    you became poor,
so that through your poverty
    we might become rich.
With our praise, O Lord,
    accept these our gifts,
and use them for the enrichment of others
    and for the glory of your name.
Based on 2 Corinthians 8. 9

673

God our Father, in your mercy accept these offerings which we now present to you with thankful hearts; and grant that our gifts may be hallowed by your blessing and used in your service; through Jesus Christ our Lord.

A flower festival 674

Lord God, Creator of the world and source of all beauty, we give thanks for the loveliness of flowers, and for the gifts of joy and hope and comfort which they convey to us.

In loving your creation, help us, our Father, to love and serve you better, and to glorify you in all your works.

We offer this prayer through Jesus Christ our Lord.

Norah Field

Before an act of dramatic worship 675

O Father, in whose presence is fullness of joy: we remember King David whose music turned men's hearts from evil and hatred to what is good; who danced before the ark of the Lord and who said "I will sing and praise the Lord": we ask you to accept this our act of worship to the honour and glory of your holy name; through Jesus Christ our Lord. *W. Temple Bourne*

A civic service 676

Lord God, we give you thanks and praise for the freedom and safety in which we live: for peaceful homes, for justice and order in our society, for standards of truth and honour, and for all our rights and privileges.

We pray for those whose work it is to maintain and extend these blessings, especially in this *borough*: all who are given authority and responsibility among us in the work of the Council, in administering the law and maintaining the peace, in education and the care of children, in planning and building, in providing both for work and for leisure.

Direct and use their influence, that together we may build a community and neighbourhood whose life does honour to your name; through Jesus Christ our Lord. *Worship Now**

See also 366-7

Holidays 677

Heavenly Father, we thank you for the holidays
  and for all times of rest and recreation.
Give refreshment of body and spirit
  to our friends who are now on holiday,
that they may return to their work and to our fellowship
  with new strength and a new vision of your love;
through Jesus Christ our Lord. *Alan Warren*

678

Lord of all good life, be with those who are now absent from
us, seeking rest and change on holiday. Keep them in safety and
renew their strength, that they may return to their homes refreshed in body, mind and spirit, for the honour and glory of your
name.

679

Heavenly Father, we thank you for all your goodness to us:
  for the wonder of your creation,
  for the happiness of holidays,
  for human love and friendship.
May we know you better through your Son Jesus,
  and live our lives to your glory
  and in the service of others,
through the power of your Holy Spirit in us,
  now and always. *Hugh Blackburne*

A general intercession 680

Almighty God, whose mercies are without number and without end, remember for good your Church: all who in every place
call on the name of the Lord, both theirs and ours; and let your
kingdom come in all the world.

Look graciously upon our country, upon this place and

neighbourhood in which we live; and give wisdom to those who exercise authority among us in Church and State, in education and industry, that we may be led in the ways of justice, truth, and freedom.

Let your blessing rest upon our families and those we love. Watch over the young; support the aged; relieve those in pain or sickness; comfort the sorrowful; succour the dying; and let your peace rest upon us all; through Jesus Christ our Lord.

Frank Colquhoun

PRAYERS FOR THE BLESSING OF A HOME

A general prayer 681

LORD Jesus Christ, who taught your apostles to bless each home they entered with the words, "Peace be to this house": we ask your blessing on the home of these your servants. Let your peace rest upon them, O Lord; keep them abiding in your love; and be with them in their going out and in their coming in, from this time forth for evermore. *Frank Colquhoun*

The dining room 682

Here, Lord Christ, we remember how you ate meals in the homes of your friends, and how on the night before your passion you met with the twelve for a last supper: may meal times in this home be hallowed by your blessing, and may food always be partaken with thankful hearts, to the glory of God the Father.

Frank Colquhoun

The kitchen 683

Heavenly Father, whose Son our Lord taught us both in word and deed that true greatness lies in serving others: sanctify all work done in this kitchen, to your glory, and enable those who serve here to do so with cheerful and willing hearts; for Jesus Christ's sake. *Frank Colquhoun*

A bedroom , **684**

Almighty God, at whose command we go forth to our work by day and take our rest by night: give to those who dwell in this home, at the ending of each day, a quiet night and the precious gift of sleep, that they may awake refreshed and renewed for your service; through Jesus Christ our Lord.

Frank Colquhoun

ACKNOWLEDGMENTS

T HE Editor wishes to express his thanks to the following for permission to reproduce or adapt material of which they are the authors, publishers, or copyright owners.

BBC Publications for prayers from the new edition (1973) of *New Every Morning* and the writers of the prayers here reproduced: the Ven. T. Dudley-Smith, Canon C. B. Naylor, the Rev. J. R. W. Stott, the Rev. J. M. Todd, the Rev. R. Tomes.

The Church Pastoral-Aid Society for prayers from *Family Worship*, and from *Prayers for Today's Church* edited by Dick Williams, and the authors of prayers from the latter: the Revs. W. F. Barker, S. H. Baynes, F. M. Best, I. D. Bunting, Cmdr. H. E. Evans, RN, the Revs. W. A. Hampton, C. M. Idle, P. Markby, A. Nugent, J. D. Searle, A. Warner, R. H. L. Williams, J. R. Worsdall.

The Saint Andrew Press for prayers from *Worship Now*, compiled by D. Cairns, I. Pitt-Watson, J. A. Whyte, T. B. Honeyman; and a prayer from *Prayers for Use in Church* by J. W. G. Masterton.

The Society for Promoting Christian Knowledge and the compilers for prayers from *A Service for Remembrance Sunday*; and for a prayer by Miss A. Milne from *Ember Prayer*.

Student Christian Movement Press for a prayer from *Contemporary Prayers for Public Worship*, edited by C. Micklem; and for prayers from *Epilogues and Prayers* by Wm. Barclay.

Oxford University Press for a prayer from *A Diocesan Service Book*, edited by L. S. Hunter.

Lutterworth Press for prayers from *Prayers at School* by J. and C. Bunch.

Geoffrey Chapman Publishers for prayers from *A Christian's Prayerbook*, edited by P. Coughlan, R. C. D. Jasper, and T. Rodrigues.

Grove Books for prayers from *Collects with the New Lectionary* by P. R. Akehurst and A. J. Bishop.

Forward Movement Publications for prayers from *Response*.

Scripture Union for prayers from *Prayers* by G. C. Robinson and S. F. Winward.

Mowbrays Publishing Division for prayers by Brother John Charles, SSF.

Church Information Office for a prayer adapted from *Church Teaching for the Junior Child*.

The Committee on Public Worship and Aids to Devotion of the Church of Scotland for prayers from *The Book of Common Order of the Church of Scotland* (Oxford University Press).

The International Committee on English in the Liturgy for a prayer from the Order of Mass.

The Rev. A. Bullen for prayers from a *Catholic Prayer Book* (Darton, Longman and Todd).

Church in Wales Publications for prayers from the *Order for the Burial of the Dead*.

Diocese of Melanesia Press for prayers from *A Book of Common Prayer in Modern English*.

Canon C. B. Naylor, the Rev. M. H. Botting, the Rev. L. F. B. Cumings, the Rev. C. M. Idle, and the Rev. J. R. Pickering, all of whom have contributed original and unpublished material.

The Right Rev. George Appleton for prayers reprinted or adapted from *In His Name* (Edinburgh House Press), *Acts of Devotion* (SPCK), *One Man's Prayers* (SPCK), and *Journey for a Soul* (Collins, Fontana Books).

The Rev. M. Saward for prayers from *Task Unfinished* (CPAS).

The Most Rev. A. M. Ramsey for two prayers adapted from his writings; the Right Rev. M. Stockwood for a prayer adapted from a diocesan letter; the Right Rev. M. A. P. Wood for various prayers; Canon A. C. Warren for prayers from *A Warwickshire Prayer Card*, and others; Mrs. Catherine Marshal for a prayer adapted from *The Prayers of Peter Marshall* (Peter Davies).

Canon H. C. Blackburne; the Rev. W. T. Bourne; Canon D. G. Caiger; Miss R. E. Cleeve; Prebendary H. Cooper; the Rev. R. Entwistle; Mrs. N. Field; Mrs. M. E. Forrester (for a prayer by the Rev. C. R. Forrester); the Rev. D. Hill; Canon G. Hyslop; the Ven. F. G. Kerr-Dineen; Canon J. Kingsnorth; the Rev. S. Linton; the Rev. A. E. Long; Mrs. A. Marshall; the Rev. L. E. H. Stephens-Hodge; Canon A. Somerset Ward (for a prayer by R. Somerset Ward); Mrs. S. Williams; Mr. D. R. Woodman.

Actors' Church Union; Advisory Council for the Church's Ministry; Cambridge Pastorate; Christian Aid; Church Missionary Society; Coventry Cathedral; Society of St. Luke the Painter; United Society for the Propagation of the Gospel.

The text of the *Revised Standard Version* and of the *New English Bible* is copyright, and due acknowledgment is made for the use of extracts from both sources.

INDEX OF SOURCES

References are to the numbers prefixed to the prayers

BIBLE REFERENCES

INDEX OF SUBJECTS

255